My Favourite Books
Non Fiction Books I've read more than once and hope to read again.

Vernon Coleman

Vernon Coleman: What the papers say

'Vernon Coleman writes brilliant books.' – The Good Book Guide
'No thinking person can ignore him.' – The Ecologist
'The calmest voice of reason.' – The Observer
'A godsend.' – Daily Telegraph
'Superstar.' – Independent on Sunday
'Brilliant!' – The People
'Compulsive reading.' – The Guardian
'His message is important.' – The Economist
'He's the Lone Ranger, Robin Hood and the Equalizer rolled into one.' – Glasgow Evening Times
'The man is a national treasure.' – What Doctors Don't Tell You
'His advice is optimistic and enthusiastic.' – British Medical Journal
'Revered guru of medicine.' – Nursing Times
'Gentle, kind and caring' – Western Daily Press
'His trademark is that he doesn't mince words. Far funnier than the usual tone of soupy piety you get from his colleagues.' – The Guardian
'Dr Coleman is one of our most enlightened, trenchant and sensitive dispensers of medical advice.' – The Observer
'I would much rather spend an evening in his company than be trapped for five minutes in a radio commentary box with Mr Geoffrey Boycott.' – Peter Tinniswood, Punch
'Hard hitting...inimitably forthright.' – Hull Daily Mail
'Refreshingly forthright.' – Liverpool Daily Post
'Outspoken and alert.' – Sunday Express
'Dr Coleman made me think again.' – BBC World Service
'Marvellously succinct, refreshingly sensible.' – The Spectator
'Probably one of the most brilliant men alive today.' – Irish Times
'King of the media docs.' – The Independent
'Britain's leading medical author.' – The Star
'Britain's leading health care campaigner.' – The Sun
'Perhaps the best known health writer for the general public in the world today.' – The Therapist
'The patient's champion.' – Birmingham Post

'A persuasive writer whose arguments, based on research and experience, are sound.' – Nursing Standard
'The doctor who dares to speak his mind.' – Oxford Mail
'He writes lucidly and wittily.' – Good Housekeeping

Books by Vernon Coleman include:

Medical
The Medicine Men
Paper Doctors
Everything You Want To Know About Ageing
The Home Pharmacy
Aspirin or Ambulance
Face Values
Stress and Your Stomach
A Guide to Child Health
Guilt
The Good Medicine Guide
An A to Z of Women's Problems
Bodypower
Bodysense
Taking Care of Your Skin
Life without Tranquillisers
High Blood Pressure
Diabetes
Arthritis
Eczema and Dermatitis
The Story of Medicine
Natural Pain Control
Mindpower
Addicts and Addictions
Dr Vernon Coleman's Guide to Alternative Medicine
Stress Management Techniques
Overcoming Stress
The Health Scandal
The 20 Minute Health Check
Sex for Everyone
Mind over Body
Eat Green Lose Weight
Why Doctors Do More Harm Than Good
The Drugs Myth

Complete Guide to Sex
How to Conquer Backache
How to Conquer Pain
Betrayal of Trust
Know Your Drugs
Food for Thought
The Traditional Home Doctor
Relief from IBS
The Parent's Handbook
Men in Bras, Panties and Dresses
Power over Cancer
How to Conquer Arthritis
How to Stop Your Doctor Killing You
Superbody
Stomach Problems – Relief at Last
How to Overcome Guilt
How to Live Longer
Coleman's Laws
Millions of Alzheimer Patients Have Been Misdiagnosed
Climbing Trees at 112
Is Your Health Written in the Stars?
The Kick-Ass A–Z for over 60s
Briefs Encounter
The Benzos Story
Dementia Myth
Medical Heretics

Psychology/Sociology
Stress Control
How to Overcome Toxic Stress
Know Yourself (1988)
Stress and Relaxation
People Watching
Spiritpower
Toxic Stress
I Hope Your Penis Shrivels Up
Oral Sex: Bad Taste and Hard To Swallow
Other People's Problems

The 100 Sexiest, Craziest, Most Outrageous Agony Column Questions (and Answers) Of All Time
How to Relax and Overcome Stress
Too Sexy To Print
Psychiatry
Are You Living With a Psychopath?

Politics and General
England Our England
Rogue Nation
Confronting the Global Bully
Saving England
Why Everything Is Going To Get Worse Before It Gets Better
The Truth They Won't Tell You...About The EU
Living In a Fascist Country
How to Protect & Preserve Your Freedom, Identity & Privacy
Oil Apocalypse
Gordon is a Moron
The OFPIS File
What Happens Next?
Bloodless Revolution
2020
Stuffed
The Shocking History of the EU
Coming Apocalypse
Covid-19: The Greatest Hoax in History
Old Man in a Chair
Endgame
Proof that Masks do more harm than Good
Covid-19: The Fraud Continues
Covid-19: Exposing the Lies
Social Credit: Nightmare on Your Street

Diaries and Autobiographies
Diary of a Disgruntled Man
Just another Bloody Year
Bugger off and Leave Me Alone
Return of the Disgruntled Man

Life on the Edge
The Game's Afoot
Tickety Tonk
Memories 1
Memories 2

Animals
Why Animal Experiments Must Stop
Fighting For Animals
Alice and Other Friends
Animal Rights – Human Wrongs
Animal Experiments – Simple Truths

General Non Fiction
How to Publish Your Own Book
How to Make Money While Watching TV
Strange but True
Daily Inspirations
Why Is Public Hair Curly
People Push Bottles Up Peaceniks
Secrets of Paris
Moneypower
101 Things I Have Learned
100 Greatest Englishmen and Englishwomen
Cheese Rolling, Shin Kicking and Ugly Tattoos
One Thing after Another
My Favourite Books

Novels (General)
Mrs Caldicot's Cabbage War
Mrs Caldicot's Knickerbocker Glory
Mrs Caldicot's Oyster Parade
Mrs Caldicot's Turkish Delight
Deadline
Second Chance
Tunnel
Mr Henry Mulligan
The Truth Kills

Revolt
My Secret Years with Elvis
Balancing the Books
Doctor in Paris
Stories with a Twist in the Tale (short stories)
Dr Bullock's Annals

The Young Country Doctor Series
Bilbury Chronicles
Bilbury Grange
Bilbury Revels
Bilbury Country
Bilbury Village
Bilbury Pie (short stories)
Bilbury Pudding (short stories)
Bilbury Tonic
Bilbury Relish
Bilbury Mixture
Bilbury Delights
Bilbury Joys
Bilbury Tales
Bilbury Days
Bilbury Memories

Novels (Sport)
Thomas Winsden's Cricketing Almanack
Diary of a Cricket Lover
The Village Cricket Tour
The Man Who Inherited a Golf Course
Around the Wicket
Too Many Clubs and Not Enough Balls

Cat books
Alice's Diary
Alice's Adventures
We Love Cats
Cats Own Annual
The Secret Lives of Cats

Cat Basket
The Cataholics' Handbook
Cat Fables
Cat Tales
Catoons from Catland

As Edward Vernon
Practice Makes Perfect
Practise What You Preach
Getting Into Practice
Aphrodisiacs – An Owner's Manual
The Complete Guide to Life

Written with Donna Antoinette Coleman
How to Conquer Health Problems between Ages 50 & 120
Health Secrets Doctors Share With Their Families
Animal Miscellany
England's Glory
Wisdom of Animals

Copyright Vernon Coleman July 2022

The right of Vernon Coleman to be identified as the author of this work has been asserted in accordance with the Copyright, Designs and Patents Act 1988.

Dedication
To Antoinette
Thank you for being you and for being with me.
I look forward to each new day only because I get to share it with you.

Introduction

I am getting old (it's something that's been coming on for a while) and as I hunted through my study, our office, the drawing room, our bedroom and the rest of the house where books are kept, for a book I knew I had, but couldn't find, I kept discovering books I'd forgotten that I had, but that I realised had affected me in some way when I'd first read them – sometimes because I'd learned something important, sometimes because I had been particularly amused or sometimes both. I put these books on one side to read again, for the optimist in me always hopes that there will be time to read just a few more dozen books.

It then slowly occurred to me (at my age it takes time for ideas to germinate) that many of the books I'd picked out are now pretty well forgotten, drowned in a tsunami of new and fashionable books, mostly written by or ghosted for, television celebrities and retired politicians.

It then also occurred to me that some of those who have been kind enough to read my books in the past might enjoy reading the old, often out of print non-fiction books which had often shaped my thinking and my outlook on life, and which they might have missed.

It occurred to me too that short descriptions of the contents of my top non-fiction books might be both entertaining and informative.

When I began the book I thought the books would choose themselves. How naïve a thought that turned out to be! It ended up being infinitely more difficult than I'd expected.

I decided that although there would inevitably be some books on the list which are classics I wanted there to be a good mix of unusual books – books which most readers might have missed. And if the authors of those books had written a number of other readable books, that would be a bonus. Although some of the books on my list are uncommon they should all be possible to find in one form or another. The one beauty of the internet is that it often makes it possible to find old books within minutes, instead of years. Throughout my life I've always enjoyed hunting around in second hand book shops but although I always found that second-hand bookshops were wonderful for finding books I didn't know I was looking for, I found that hunting for a specific book often involved visits to several dozen bookshops and a hunt extending over several years. The internet has obviously changed that. So, for example, it took me many months to find all the volumes of James Agate's 'Ego' diaries on the internet, but I doubt if I would have ever found them all if I had relied upon scrabbling around the dusty shelves of second-hand book shops.

This has been a surprisingly dangerous book to write.

I have over the years bought tens of thousands of books (and received many thousands of books sent for review). Sadly, and regrettably, I have over the years donated thousands of books to charity shops (and I've given many boxfuls to second-hand bookshops which were struggling to survive) but there are still many thousands left. (I haven't counted them and I don't intend to do so.)

The result is that our home in Bilbury is full of books (only the boiler room, the boot room, the butler's pantry and the bathrooms are largely free of books – though I confess I did have two book shelves put up in my bathroom) and we ran out of shelf space a long time ago. The result is that books sit in precarious piles and, having absolutely no patience at all, I repeatedly tried pulling a selected volume out from the middle, or more likely near the bottom, of a teetering four or five foot high stack of books. If my foot work wasn't nifty enough most of the books, and quite possibly an adjacent pile, would come crashing down on parts of me that weren't created for being attacked by battalions of books.

Still, in the end I got there: I found my non-fiction books.

It is, of course, a very personal selection, and I don't expect anyone to be captivated by every book in this selection (it would be strange if they were) but if you are anything like me you will be delighted to find news of half a dozen books you hadn't previously discovered and, in crude footballing parlance, be over the moon to find a dozen. This isn't offered as the definitive list of non-fiction books. It is merely a list of non-fiction books which I found captivating, informative and delightful. I hope you will find my notes encouraging and invigorating. The only criterion was that the books on the list had to be available in an English language edition. Some are definitely not available in paperback but hardback editions should not be too hard to find.

I have always been a voracious reader (perhaps because I was an only child who quickly found companionship in books and almost as quickly discovered the joy of finding that an author I liked had written many books). Over the years, I have found that some of the most rewarding volumes are those which were written years ago and which are now out of print and largely forgotten – but often still available on the internet, of course.

William Morris advised us to have nothing in our homes which is not beautiful or useful and the same thought can be applied, in a slightly modified form, to books. 'Read nothing which is not entertaining or informative', might be a useful guiding principle. The books in this selection have been picked because they are either enormously entertaining or exceptionally illuminating or, preferably, both.

Finally, I apologise to those books which didn't make the hundred. (Most of the authors concerned are no longer with us so I feel I should offer my apologies to the books, which are.)

I had to stop somewhere but I could have easily made this list 'My 200 Favourite Non-Fiction books'.

I didn't include any books from the excellent King Penguin series or the Britain in Pictures series though I have complete sets of both series and almost all the books in both series are well worth finding and reading. And I haven't included any dictionaries, thesauruses, encyclopaedias or reference books. Somehow, I missed out both Hans Selye's classic books on stress, the first of which was published in 1955, and W.B.Cannon's book on physiology entitled 'The Wisdom of the Body' which was published in 1932. Those two didn't make the cut because although they're important to me, and played a big part in guiding my thinking about medicine, I suspect they might be of less interest to the general reader. Shamefully I didn't find room for H.M.Stanley's massive books about Livingstone and the Dark Continent, and nor did Boswell's 'Life of Johnson' make my list of books. I now have no idea how they came to be left out. 'The Worst Journey in the World', Apsley Cherry-Garrard's classic book about the Captain Scott expedition to the South Pole, didn't make my list because I found it just too endlessly depressing for me to want to read again (one of the criteria for selection). Clifford Irving's book 'Project Octavio' (about how he pretended to be Howard Hughes and sold his autobiography to a publisher) nearly made the cut, but didn't, nor did William Donaldson's large, unusual dictionary 'Brewer's Rogues, Villains and Eccentrics'. (At one point I wrote an entry for the 'Henry Root' letters, written under the Henry Root pseudonym but authored by Donaldson, but the entry, like numerous others was eventually squeezed out.) I decided against Truman Capote's 'In Cold Blood' for no good reason that I can think of other than that it's just too darned gloomy and manipulative and didn't satisfy either of my two criteria. I decided that Vance Packard's 'Hidden Persuaders' (a masterpiece about the advertising industry) is rather dated and not fascinating enough to merit re-reading (but still well worth reading if you haven't read it and want to know more about how advertisers use psychology to sell products) and Alvin Toffler's huge bestseller 'Future Shock' missed my list for the same reason. John Buchan wrote a number of good history books, particularly one about 'The Massacre of Glencoe', which is especially revealing, but they're rather specialised so they didn't get in either. (I did, however, include a book which he edited – 'A History of English Literature'.) I thought for a while about Rachel Carson, whose book 'Silent Spring' triggered people to be concerned about the environment, but decided that none of her books pass the 'do I want to re-read this book' test. Henry Fielding's marvellous and incredibly readable small book 'Journal of a Voyage to Lisbon' was squeezed out at the last minute when I decided that I really couldn't leave Mark Twain out of my selection since his travel books and his massive autobiography are essential non-fiction reading and valuable parts of his canon. And then I remembered Preston Sturges and decided that Mr Twain is well enough known, and that his books could manage quite well without a boost from me (though, ludicrously and sadly, even Twain is now subject to bans and censorship). So out went Twain and in came Sturges. My selection took me twice as long to write as it should have done because I was continually writing pieces about books I liked and then replacing those pieces with essays about books I found on my shelves and realised I liked even more or which I thought were, for some reason, more relevant to the book. Several times I remembered books I liked and then, when I couldn't find them, bought new copies to write about.

 I could have messed around with my list for another decade. I realised, as I wrote this, that I didn't have anything by or about W.S.Gilbert – the co-author of the Savoy Operas. But with all books of this type there comes a time when the author has to say: 'Enough! This is the best I can do today – though if I remade this list tomorrow it would probably be different. The books I selected aren't necessarily the most beautifully written, but they are, I think, books which can now be read or re-read with advantage.

Finally, finally I should point out that my collection of books is not listed in any particular order. I could, I suppose, have put them in an A to Z list. But should they be in A to Z order according to title or in an A to Z list according to author's name? I could have put them in date order, according to when they were published – but why? And I didn't want to put them in a list like a hit parade, because since I've selected every one of them they'd all be at number one. So the books are listed entirely at random – as I picked them off the shelves and wrote about them.

These are, I hope, books which you may have missed but which you will be glad I told you about.

Vernon Coleman
Bilbury 2022

Roche versus Adams
Stanley Adams
First published 1984
Stanley Adams' book really plucked at my heart strings when it was first published.

Hoffman-la-Roche, the manufacturer of benzodiazepine tranquillisers such as Valium and Librium and, at the time the world's largest supplier of vitamins, had been a target of mine since before I wrote my first book 'The Medicine Men' in 1975.

I had, since around 1970, been a staunch critic of Roche because of the unbridled and unfettered enthusiasm with which the company promoted its benzodiazepines. (My recent book 'The Benzos Story' summaries my early research into the perils of those over-sold, over-prescribed and over-swallowed drugs.)

Adams was a well-rewarded, senior employee at Roche. In 1973 he became aware that Roche was price fixing and controlling the world wide vitamin market.

When Switzerland (where Roche was based) signed a free market agreement with what was then called the Common Market (now known as the European Union), Adams approached the Market's commission in charge of competition laws. And, after having blown a rather loud whistle, he left Roche and put his life savings into a pig farm in Italy.

In 1974, Adams and his family crossed into Switzerland for a New Year's Eve family celebration. That was when his nightmare started.

Adams was arrested, put into solitary confinement and tried for industrial espionage and treason. All this because he had told the Common Market about Roche's dirty dealings and the Common Market had run to Roche and told them of his whistle blowing.

Marilene Adams (Stanley's wife) wasn't allowed to communicate with her husband and was told that he faced up to 20 years in prison. Despairing, she committed suicide. Almost unbelievably, Adams wasn't told for days and was refused to permission to attend her funeral.

After being released on bail Adams went home to look after his three daughters and his pig farm. But bank facilities previously arranged were suddenly 'not forthcoming' and Adams went bankrupt and lost his farm.

In 1979, on Christmas Eve, Adams was again arrested and imprisoned.

He later fought for compensation from what had by now become the European Economic Community and eventually had a tenth of his debts paid. When released from prison Adams fled to England.

That, in the proverbial nutshell, is the horrific story told in 'Roche versus Adams'. Adams, the honest whistle-blower, was damned near destroyed by Roche and the European Union.

After I read this book, I made sure that I paid off my mortgage as quickly as possible and never again borrowed any money from anyone.

Fog Facts
Larry Beinhart
First published 2005

Larry Beinhart is the author of the novel 'American Hero' which was turned into a magnificently funny film called 'Wag the Dog', starring Dustin Hoffman and Robert De Niro. (Although book and film are both excellent the film doesn't much resemble the book).

'Fog Facts', subtitled 'Searching for Truth in the Land of Spin', is an exploration of the way politicians are forever spinning, and journalists are forever cooperating in their deceit – enabling them in exploring the ever expanding margins of global corruption. Between them, politicians and journalists have filled the world with false flags and mis-directions – creating an impenetrable 'fog of facts' which make it difficult for anyone to find the truth, or to concentrate on the truth if they are astute enough to find it.

Here's the last paragraph of the book:

'This is a practical issue. Not merely a moral one. If you drive around in the fog, you must go very slowly. Americans like to go fast. When you speed in the fog, eventually you crash into something.'

I think the title is terrible, and the book would have done much better with a different one, but the content is riveting and crucial –

especially in view of what has happened in the years which have followed the book's publication.

Readers who find this book fascinating will also enjoy (if that is the right word) 'Presstitutes' by Dr Udo Ulfkotte and 'The Press' by A.J.Liebling. (A 'presstitute', by the way, is defined as someone, either a journalist or a television talking head, who will print whatever they are paid to write and print or say whatever they are paid to say on television or radio. We have seen an explosion in the number of 'presstitutes' in action in the years after 2019.)

Birds Useful and Harmful
Otto Herman and J.A.Owen
First published 1909

There are many unusual, almost eccentric, books on my shelves but I've never been interested in deliberately, self-consciously eccentric books, designed to capture the Christmas market. Every year publishers produce armfuls of odd books which will gather a giggle from the recipient, be looked at for a few minutes and then tossed into the bag for the charity shop. 'Birds Useful and Harmful' is definitely not one of those.

The book was commissioned by M.Daranyi, the Royal Hungarian Minister who was in charge of his country's agricultural interests. He wanted a book to give to farmers, landowners, fruit growers and gardeners, to provide them with information about birds. He wanted a book that would help them decide which birds to welcome and which to regard with suspicion or even loathing.

Beautifully illustrated with black and white drawings, 'Birds Useful and Harmful' is packed with glorious anecdotes and titbits of information. The tone of the book is, thankfully, generous to birds. So, for example, in writing about the kingfisher the authors note that they would 'not call a bird hurtful because it seeks the food which its creator intended it to eat'.

Although it could be dismissed as a reference book 'Birds Useful and Harmful' is wonderfully readable, sympathetic and full of charm.

Young Emma
W.H.Davies
1980 (posthumously)
Best known for his writing about his early life as a tramp (as in 'The Autobiography of a Super Tramp' and for the lines 'What is this life if, full of care, We have no time to stand and stare'), Davies had been a bachelor (though certainly no misogynist) until his 50s. At that point, living in a squalid bedsit near Marble Arch he realised that although he was popular in literary circles, largely because he was famous as a literary oddity, this was a temporary state. He realised that the people who lionised him would drop him in an instant when a suitable replacement appeared.

And so, he decided to make two changes to his life. He would find a wife and move to the country.

Although there were a number of 'society' ladies with whom he could have made a profitable alliance, he chose to look for a bride on the streets of London and found a prostitute called Emma. She was pregnant and she had venereal disease but he fell in love with her and married her.

This book is the story of their love.

'Young Emma' was written in 1924 but it wasn't published for 56 years. Davies died in 1940 but it was only after Emma's death in 1979 that the book was finally published. It is an incredibly touching story of love, loyalty and commitment.

The Compleat Anger
Izaac Walton
First published 1653
Since I am a vegetarian, and have been one for half my life, is may seem odd to include a book about fishing. But Walton's book satisfies both my criteria. It is a fascinating instruction book and it is surprisingly entertaining to read. Some of the book is written in prose and some is in verse. It is a very personal book, written as a dialogue between friends, and at the start of the book the fisherman, the falconer and the hunter discuss and commend the qualities of their various recreations.

Walton was brought up in Staffordshire in the Midlands, although he moved to London while still a boy. His fishing was done in a variety of English rivers. He was a friend and fishing companion of John Donne and wrote a biography of Donne, though it is his book on fishing for which he is remembered.

As a boy Walton was apprenticed to a draper, though later he acquired his own shop in London.

At the front of book (I am using the fifth edition which was published in 1676) Walton points out that in writing his book he has made a 'recreation of a recreation' and in a note which is addressed 'To the reader of this discourse but especially to the honest angler' he writes:

'I have in several places mixed, not any scurrility, but some innocent, harmless mirth, of which, if thou be a severe, sour-complexioned man, then I here disallow thee to be a competent judge; for divines say, there are offences given, and offences not given but taken.'

And then, a little further on, he writes:

'But I think all that love this game may here learn something that may be worth their money, if they be not poor and needy men: and in case they be, I then wish them to forbear to buy it; for I write not to get money, but for pleasure, and this Discourse boasts of no more, for I hate to promise much, and deceive the Reader.'

At the end of what is, in effect, his introduction to the book Walton concludes:

'When I have told the reader, that in this fifth impression there are many enlargements, gathered both by my own observation, and the communication with friends, I shall stay him no longer than to wish him a rainy evening to read this following Discourse; and that if he be an honest Angler, the east wind may never blow when he goes a-fishing.'

With a copy of Walton's book in one pocket and a copy of Gilbert White's masterpiece 'The Natural History of Selborne' (also in my list) in the other, a traveller need never be bored.

Need your Doctor be so useless?
Andrew Malleson
First published 1973

Although he was born in Britain, Dr Andrew Malleson was working in Toronto, Canada, as a psychiatrist, when he wrote this book. He had worked as a GP in London and in Germany as a medical army officer and had gone round the world twice as a ship's surgeon.

I found Malleson's book inspirational, incredibly well-researched and comprehensive as well as witty and readable. Malleson was one of the first doctors willing, let alone able, to assess the values of modern medical practices. He looked at the way that doctors often fail their patients and how they influence, often with malign intent, the way that politicians, journalists and commentators look at illness and medical care.

It was Hippocrates, of course, who taught us that doctors should be useful to patients and should do them no harm. Malleson reminds his readers of this and asks how useful doctors and medicines really are today.

'Need your doctor be so useless' is gloriously iconoclastic. Malleson points out that (in 1973) health care was becoming institutionalised and argues that a changeover from hospital to community based health care would prove advantageous and make health services more efficient, less expensive and more pleasant to use.

Sadly, his advice was ignored and the trend has taken doctors (and patients) in precisely the opposite direction – with disastrous results.

Under an English Heaven
Donald E.Westlake
First published 1972

Donald E.Westlake is one of my favourite novelists. Under his own name he wrote what publishers (who love to label books and authors) usually refer to as 'comedy thrillers'. But, like many other successful authors, he wrote under a variety of pen names, the best known of which was Richard Stark. As Stark he wrote a shelf full of thrillers about a career criminal called Parker. I don't think many (if any) authors have had more of their books filmed – and in a high percentage of cases turned into successful movies.

But this is a book about non-fiction writing and Westlake's

curious book 'Under an English Heaven' is a marvellous foray into a usually unexplored genre.

On March 19th 1969, the tiny obscure Caribbean island of Anguilla was invaded by Great Britain. Over 300 marines and paratroopers arrived on the island, taken there by two frigates and several helicopters. The soldiers were accompanied (and this must have been the bit which attracted Westlake's attention) by fifty London policemen.

The invasion was given the code name Operation Sheepskin and the island was captured with no resistance and no casualties. It was described by the British, rather starved of such things at the time, as a famous victory.

The British invaded because the Anguillans had been unhappy about being governed from St Kitts. A local conflict somehow turned into a revolt. The rebel flag was the Union Jack.

The invasion lasted over two years and ended in confusion, though the British invaders built schools and roads and started a democratic election process – so their presence wasn't a complete waste of time.

Westlake became involved in the Anguillan affair because he felt the reality was in flagrant and unwarranted competition with his own comic fiction. The book is dedicated 'to anyone anywhere who has ever believed anything that any Government ever said about anything…'

We were young and carefree
Laurent Fignon
First published 2010
I really don't know why but I have been an enthusiastic follower of the Tour de France ever since the days when Eddie Merx seemed to win most of the stages and most of the jerseys.

My favourite rider of all time is Laurent Fignon, simply because he was the most exciting to watch. He was alone among professional cyclists in being charismatic, flamboyant and unpredictable. He rode like a hero; always wanting to take the race by the scruff of the neck, always attacking and making dramatic moves.

Fignon died young (he was just 50) but his later years were in some ways tragic because he was remembered by millions as the man who lost the Tour de France by just eight seconds (still the narrowest margin). Fignon had been leading the Tour by quite a comfortable margin but the final stage was a time trial, with cyclists competing against the clock. Fignon's main rival was an American cyclist called Greg Lemond.

Everything went wrong for Fignon on that day. He was ill, he nearly didn't get to the start line because his car wouldn't start and he rode an ordinary, fairly old-fashioned racing bike while Lemond used a bicycle with special handlebars – which probably gave him a considerable advantage.

Losing the Tour de France (a three week long stage race) by just eight seconds haunted Fignon, who had won the race twice at a very early age, and he retired far too early. He admits in the book that he used recreational drugs but he left the sport early, in part at least, because he refused to use any of the doping techniques which were rapidly becoming essential for anyone hoping to win a stage, let alone the race.

This is a sad book, a touching book and an emotional book in which the author bares his soul and reveals his inner torments. But it is also a funny book, an intriguing book and the best sporting autobiography I've ever read. Fignon won over eighty titles and was a great sportsman but his demons were constantly chasing him down.

Between Meals: An Appetite for Paris
A.J.Liebling
First published 1959
A.J.Liebling has been a favourite author of mine since I bought a paperback copy of this book from Sylvia Beech's bookshop Shakespeare and Co, opposite the Notre Dame in Paris.

Liebling was a writer for the New Yorker magazine back in the days when it was arguably the greatest English language magazine in the world, and hadn't yet become what I now regard as a miserable mouthpiece for conspirators and left wing lunatics.

The extraordinary Harold Ross was the editor and contributors included James Thurber and E.B.White. The cartoons were sharp, witty and often worth clipping and keeping.

Many of Liebling's articles for the New Yorker have been collected and published in book form. For example, 'The Road Back to Paris' is a collection of idiosyncratic reports from Europe during the Second World War. Liebling was no one's idea of a foreign correspondent, let alone a war correspondent. He was overweight, myopic and had bad feet. But he wrote about ordinary men and women, interviewed soldiers in the trenches and described his own endless searches for decent meals in wartime Paris. Liebling had been sent to France to replace Janet Flanner, the magazine's usual (and legendary) correspondent in France who had to return to the US. (Flanner's collected columns are also available in book form and are well worth reading, though they do not have Liebling's effortless, personal charm.)

But my favourite Liebling book, which was his last and which was the one which I see from a pencilled note on the flyleaf I bought from Shakespeare and Co for 49 francs, is 'Between Meals: An Appetite for Paris'. It is a book I have read many times and it never fails to enthral and delight.

It is, as you might expect from the title, a book about eating in Paris. But it is far more than it sounds. It is a book about wonderful meals, about marvellous wines, great friendships, magnificent chefs, gourmands, gourmets and a few gluttons too. It is a book about meals that go on for hours and consist of seemingly endless courses. It is a book about luncheons which seem to merge effortlessly into dinners, with scarcely a defining break between the two. It is a book about the city of Paris and the Parisians. But most of all it is a most extraordinary, always memorable, ever-engaging autobiography. It is wise, charming and funny and it is, and always will be, one of my very favourite non-fiction books.

Through Wood and Dale
James Lee-Milne
First published 1998

The best diaries are written in the Samuel Pepys style: indiscreet, gossipy, perceptive, outrageous, opinionated, personal and honest at all costs. Good examples of published diaries are surprisingly difficult to find. Too many diaries written by (or ghosted for) celebrities are dull, precious, self-aware and often little more than a smorgasbord of shared meals and endless name dropping. Some look as if they are little more than appointment diaries. Alan Clark's diaries were much praised for the political gossip and for the indiscretions they contained but I don't believe they were well enough written to entertain generations to come.

James Lee-Milne's diaries contain gossip and indiscretions, and a good deal of name dropping because he was a snob, and rather obsessed with the aristocracy. But his diaries are charming and curiously enhanced by his snobbishness. His delight in referring to a Duke by his first name is curiously childish but engaging.

Lees-Milne was a writer, though his memorable books are his diaries, but he also worked for the National Trust, visiting grand country houses whose owners, tired of all the costs involved in keeping roofs watertight, grounds tidied and rooms warmed, wanted to hand them over to the Trust. Many just couldn't cope with several dozen bedrooms and, having flogged all the saleable art, were desperate to move into a neat four bedroom home with affordable central heating. Astonishingly, owners of large houses who wanted to hand over their responsibilities were expected to give a dowry to help towards the upkeep of the house, grange, manor or palace which they no longer wanted.

'Through Wood and Dale' is my favourite of the Lees-Milne diaries because it comes after earlier companion volumes with which Lees-Milne's many friends were variously delighted, shocked or mortified by the author's indiscretions, revelations and previously privately stored acid insults. The odd thing is that most of the people he wrote about seemed happy to stay friends – quite possibly because they yearned for the immortality they hoped would be theirs if they continued to be pilloried and lampooned in the Lees-Milne diaries.

Few diarists have ever been as observant or had such a refined sense of the absurd. James Lees-Milne is never self-conscious and never pompous.

A Family at Sea

Denys Val Baker
First published 1981
One of the modest joys in life is finding an excellent book by a previously undiscovered author and one of the great joys is discovering that the previously undiscovered author had hitherto written a whole series of books, all also previously undiscovered.

I discovered Denys Val Baker years ago and was never disappointed by any of his books. He wrote marvellously simple, evocative books about his homes, his family and his life. If you met him you'd end up in one of his books. After a few pages you feel you know Val Baker and his family. You become part of the family, welcomed into his world.

'A Family at Sea' is a little different to the other books in the series in that (no surprise, this) it describes the family's adventures in an elderly converted fishing boat called MFV Sanu.

Val Baker, his wife and six children cruise the Mediterranean and Northern Europe. They travel along the Seine to the heart of Paris, sail round the Western Isles, sail through the Dutch canals and visit the Greek Islands, Sicily, Malta, Elba and the Riviera.

And, of course, things go wrong.

As reality television producers have reminded us so vividly it is only when things go wrong that we are properly hooked. If there isn't a flood, or a storm, or a fire or some other disaster then our interest will not be awakened – though we do like things to be sorted out conveniently and happily in the end.

As they are in this book, of course.

Val Baker and company are battered by storms and a cyclone. The pumps stop working and the boat fills with water. It sinks twice.

Is that enough for you?

This is travel writing that means something.

And if you don't much like the idea of messing around in boats, the other Val Baker books are marvellous entertainment.

The Story of San Michele
Alex Munthe
First published 1929
Even Alex Munthe admitted that he had difficulty in classifying

'The Story of San Michele'.

It is partly an autobiography (Munthe was a doctor who writes wisely, vividly and compassionately about his patients); it is partly a book about the people he knew (escaped convicts, a grave digger, a harlot, various government officials and a Contessa); it is partly a travel book (about the island where he bought a house); it is partly an adventure book (he is at one point buried under an avalanche) and, not surprisingly, it is a book about San Michele where Munthe eventually made his home.

Every page seems to bring surprises.

So, for example: 'Late the following afternoon as I was crawling among the ruins…in search of the corpse of the Swedish Consul, I was suddenly confronted with a soldier pointing his rifle at me. I was arrested and taken to the nearest post.'

Since Dr Munthe failed to find a satisfactory classification for his book, I am not going to try: it would be presumptuous even to think of it. Maybe the whole thing is fiction. Who knows? Who cares? I have read 'The Story of San Michele more than once and I hope to read it again. Whatever sort of book it is, it is a classic.

The Story of My Heart
Richard Jefferies
First published 1883

The first thing to make clear is that, despite the title, this is not an autobiography.

So, what is it?

It is, I suppose, an autobiography of the soul; it is inspirational; it is intense and, in a way, it is the story of a man making his peace with his God. It is an iconoclastic book about beauty and it is a book Jefferies had been thinking about for 17 years.

Jefferies was a sick man (he had tuberculosis) when he wrote 'The Story of My Heart' (though he lived another few years – dying in 1887) and in a way it is a prayer by a man contemplating his own mortality. It is a book of memories and certainties but it is also a book of contradictions, questions and mysteries.

Jefferies himself described the book as a confession in which he stands face to face with nature and with the unknown.

It's not an easy book to read but then it can't have been an easy book to write.

The Life of the Fly
J Henri Fabre
First published 1913
I can confidently say that this is one of the strangest books I've ever read. The full title is: 'The Life of the Fly: The Insects' Homer with which are interspersed some chapters of autobiography.'

The really curious thing is that it appears to have been the translator, Alexander Teixeira de Mattos who decided to intersperse M.Fabre's essays on diptera, from his book 'Souvenirs Entomologiques', with autobiographical essays from his book 'Souvenirs'. This was done, apparently, 'in order to make the dimensions uniform with those of the other volumes in the series'.

Now, I find that odd enough in itself, but the really strange thing is that chapters about bluebottles, maggots and the grey flesh flies are mixed in with chapters of M.Fabre's autobiography and the really, really bizarre thing is that the whole thing works. And it works because the caddis worm and the bumble bee fly were such an important part of M.Fabre's life. Serendipity works.

The book finishes with M.Fabre being awarded the Legion of Honour, given a huge pile of books as a gift and a roll of 1,200 francs to cover the expenses incurred in travelling to collect his ribbon.

This is a strange book and, I suppose, M. Fabre led a strange life. But the strangest thing is that it all works beautifully: it's an unforgettable book.

Will Pickles of Wensleydale: The Life of a Country Doctor
John Pemberton
First published 1970
Every first year medical student should read this book. Every newly qualified doctor should read it again. Every nurse should read it. Every health service or hospital administrator should read it.

Everyone even vaguely interested in health care (and that is surely all of us) should read it.

Sadly, almost no one will.

Will Pickles was a family doctor who worked in the North Riding of Yorkshire in the first half of the twentieth century. Dr Pickles realised that, as a country doctor, he had a special opportunity to study the spread of disease and at the age of 42, he began recording the incidence of infectious disease in his practice. He didn't have a computer, of course. He used a notebook. He tracked the spread of disease in his practice, jotting down details of meetings in the pub or at the local fete. If he knew that a disease had spread between individuals involved in a clandestine affair he would make a tactful, confidential note of that. And he did this for the next 25 years.

In the first 20 of those years he meticulously recorded 6,808 cases of infectious disease – including influenza, diarrhoea and vomiting, chickenpox, mumps, whooping cough, scarlet fever, hepatitis, lobar pneumonia and measles. Because he lived among his patients, and knew them well, Dr Pickles could trace the source and spread of epidemics in the dale where he lived.

Professor John Pemberton worked as a locum with Dr Pickles on nine occasions and knew him well. The love, the friendship and respect shines through on every page.

Dr Pickles himself wrote a magnificent book entitled 'Epidemiology in Country Practice'. It is a valued book on my shelves and highly recommended.

Pickles was one of the world's most significant epidemiologists and it is a tragedy that he is not more widely remembered with both respect and affection.

'A gypsy woman driving a caravan into a village in the summer twilight,' he wrote, 'a sick husband in the caravan, a faulty pump at which she proceeded to wash her dirty linen and my first and only serious epidemic of typhoid left me with a lasting impression of the unique opportunities of the country doctor for the investigation of infectious disease.'

And just as Dr John Snow had so memorably arranged to have the Broad Street pump handle removed (to prevent the spread of cholera) so Dr Pickles had the handle chained to the pump. 'And there were no primary cases,' he declared in triumph.

Pickles believed that country GPs had a special opportunity

because they 'tend to remain in one practice and to become part of their district.' Also he wrote: 'we do not readily retire…retirement makes for early death.'

The tragedy is that so few other doctors followed the example Dr Pickles set. It was his ambition that they would. 'The object of this book,' he wrote, 'is primarily an attempt to stimulate other country doctors to keep records of epidemic disease.'

So, why didn't they?

It was, I suspect, the abundance of boring bureaucratic paperwork that suffocated doctors.

But Pickles provided us with valuable information about the spread of a host of infectious diseases including chickenpox, dysentery and measles. It is our tragedy that his work has been largely forgotten.

Before Hansard
Horace King
First published 1968

It is well known that the official record of Parliamentary business in Britain has, for over two centuries, been recorded in a publication called Hansard.

But although Hansard hasn't always been there, Parliament has kept a daily record of everything that has been said and done. The record goes back to the reign of Edward VI and was variously known as the Rolls of Parliament and the Journal.

In 'Before Hansard', Horace Maybury King (who was himself an MP and a speaker of the House of Commons), provides an illuminating, funny and astonishing selection from Parliament's history.

From the days of Queen Elizabeth I onwards, the early records are supplemented with material from diaries and other contemporary records. Some of the events recorded were trivial, some sublime, some ridiculous and many were a vital record of democracy's progress.

In 1787 (to take a year at random), the king (in his speech to Parliament) announced that: 'A plan has been formed, by my direction, for transporting a number of convicts in order to remove the inconveniences which arise from the crowded state of the gaols in different parts of the kingdom'.

Two months later, in the same year, it was announced that the Government had imposed duties of '£1.10.10 on every hundredweight of Elephants' Teeth and two shillings on every pound of Human Hair, imported into this country'.

How could anyone go through life without knowing that?

Down the Garden Path
Beverley Nichols
First published in 1934

It is difficult to express just how popular the author Beverley Nichols was in the 1920s and 1930s. Also well known as a journalist his sense of self-importance and love of good living would have guaranteed him several million followers on social media.

Much of his journalism is lost, of course, though some of his interviews and profiles still exist in collections of essays and his work on gardening remains a delight. His novels haven't lasted terribly well but his autobiographies have retained their sense of joy and were sold in such huge quantities that they are easy to find in whatever second-hand bookshops remain and online. Beverley Nichols wrote gloriously happy books about himself, his houses, his cats and his friends but it is his books about his cottage 'Always' which are most worth reading.

'Down the Garden path' is the first in the series (sequels 'A Thatched Roof in a Village' and 'A Village in a Valley' are equally charming) and like many of his books it is illustrated by Rex Whistler.

Nichols writes about his home, his garden, the villagers and his visitors and it is a safe bet that most of the conversations and incidents he describes in delightful detail never actually happened in precisely the way he describes. I really don't care. The reader is invited to relax in another world, in simpler times, and Nichols shares (almost) everything with great generosity. (He was a homosexual and knew that sharing that bit of news would have killed his sales.)

Every few years I walk my fingers through my shelves,

rediscover Beverley Nichols and re-immerse myself in his wonderful world.

Harpo Speaks
Harpo Marx
First published in 1961
I've always loved the Marx Brothers and, like many fans, I had a very large, soft spot for Harpo, the silent clown – the only one of the brothers (and probably the only film star) who could walk down the street and not be bothered by autograph hunters. As he points out 'people don't recognise me out of costume' and 'the public has never heard my voice'. (He didn't speak because he had a rather deep, slow way of talking which didn't fit with his stage persona.)

The book is full of wonderful anecdotes.

My favourite is the story about how, on the way to a theatre to watch a film, he bought thirty dollars' worth of black jelly beans (as a boy he'd only ever been able to afford a penny's worth). Sitting in the theatre the huge bag burst and slippery jelly beans rolled down the aisle, causing absolute chaos. The manager of the cinema had to stop the picture and turn on the lights to allow the ushers to shovel up the beans.

When told by Chico that prohibition was coming, Harpo filled his cellar with booze. Only afterwards did he work out that since he wasn't a big drinker he had bought enough alcohol to last him until he was 525 years old.

Invited to be the first American artist to perform in Moscow, he was stopped by customs who insisted that he opened his luggage. In his trunk they discovered his red wigs, false beards, bottles marked poison, two revolvers and a huge number of knives. They opened his harp case and insisted he play to prove that he was a harpist. His hands were so cold that he couldn't play anything recognisable.

Harpo played the piano in a whorehouse, he gambled with Nick the Greek, sat on the floor with Greta Garbo, played ping pong with George Gershwin, golfed with Sam Snead and Ben Hogan, sat at the Algonquin round table with Dorothy Parker and Robert Benchley, enjoyed the company of Somerset Maugham on the Riviera and was thrown out of the casino in Monte Carlo. And he and his brothers made some of the funniest films ever produced.

What a life!

Who the Devil made It?
Peter Bogdanovich
First published 1997

Anyone who has the slightest interest in movies really should pick up Bogdanovich's masterpiece – though arthritis sufferers and the elderly might need help because it is a huge, heavy book.

The idea behind the book is very simple.

Bogdanovich interviewed 16 legendary film directors including Allan Dwan (who made more than 400 movies, including silent one reelers, created the first screen idol – Douglas Fairbanks – and discovered many stars). Dwan describes that he became a film director because the original director had been away on a drinking binge for two weeks. Having no idea what to do, Dwan asked the actors for advice. They handed him a megaphone and told him to yell 'Come on!' or 'Action'.

'The cameraman will start turning the camera,' he was told, 'and we'll ride over the hill.'

Other directors interviewed include Robert Aldrich, George Cukor, Howard Hawks, Alfred Hitchcock, Fritz Lang, Sidney Lumet, Otto Preminger, Josef von Sternberg and Raoul Walsh.

The book works well because Bogdanovich (himself a successful film director of films – including What's Up Doc? And The Last Picture Show) knew exactly what questions to ask. And all the directors he interviewed trusted him enough to answer honestly.

It is the best book ever written on film making – full of wonderful anecdotes.

Bogdanovich also wrote 'Who the Hell's In it?' in which he publishes details of in-depth conversations with Cary Grant, James Stewart, Audrey Hepburn, Bogart, Brando, Chaplin, John Wayne, James Cagney, Frank Sinatra, Dean Martin, Jerry Lewis, Jack Lemmon, Marlene Dietrich, Marilyn Monroe and more.

It was Bogdanovich who related this wonderful story about Clint Eastwood.

Eastwood was making a film and asked the director if it was

necessary to do a scene setting up the fact that the character he was playing was fast with a gun.

'They know you're fast, Clint,' said the director.

And that, of course, is the secret of the star system. A star brings baggage with him that the director has to respect. It was for that reason, for example, that Hitchcock knew that he couldn't have Cary Grant play the 'baddie' in a movie.

British Music Hall – an Illustrated History
Richard Antony Baker
First published 2014

All modern popular entertainment can be traced back to the music hall. First truly popular towards the end of the 19th century, music hall was at its best and most popular in the years up until the First World War.

A hundred years earlier the music hall tradition had started in inns and taverns where special rooms had to be added on to cater for the crowds. Eventually, special theatres were built and songs and acts written and developed for the new venues. Popular artists soon became famous and enormously rich. Unlike television performers, who constantly need new material, they could perform the same script and tell the same jokes, night after night as they toured the country. John Read, for example, sang his own song 'Grandmother's Chair' an estimated 10,000 to 12,000 times. (J.B.Priestley's novel 'Good Companions' tells the story of the touring troupe better than anyone.)

Music hall belonged to what used to be known as the working classes, and it was largely from the working classes that the first big stars such as Marie Lloyd and Little Titch emerged. By the 1930s, the cinema had appeared and had taken over from the music hall. Gracie Fields and George Formby Jr, who had originally found success in the music halls, then became two of the biggest film stars in the world.

The Money Game
Adam Smith

First published 1968
I have a huge collection of books about finance in general and investment in particular. Some of the books date back 100 years and some are very recent. This is the best. And I've read it several times.

Two things about money occurred to me many decades ago.

First, freedom and independence grow considerably if you have a little money put away. This is especially true for those who earn their living without the comfort of a 'proper' job with an employer, rights and a pension.

Second, the finance industry (banks, investment companies, pension companies, advisors and so on) is ruthlessly dishonest and can only rarely be trusted. My default position has always been distrust.

Of all those books about money on my shelves 'The Money Game' is the one I've read more often than any other. (It is important to point out the 'Adam Smith' in question is a pen name. The author was a financier called George Goodman and, other than the similarity in name, nothing to do with the Scottish economist famous for a far less readable tome.)

'The Money Game' is brilliant for two reasons.

First, it is full of solid, practical, valuable, easy to understand information.

Second, it has a quality that is rare in books about money: it is charming, funny and extremely readable.

It is, indeed, a book that should be read by everyone with two halfpennies to rub together. And by anyone who'd like to have two halfpennies to rub together.

I don't know how much personal finance is taught in schools these days. When I was young they taught us absolutely nothing about money. But if every 18-year-old was given a copy of this to read there would be far less ignorance, far fewer successful con artists and far fewer online scams, and pension providers would have a far harder time of it when cheating their customers.

'Adam Smith' wrote several other books. 'Paper Money' and 'Supermoney' are excellent, but none of his other books is as magical as this one.

Preston Sturges
Preston Sturges
First published 1990

This is an autobiography and a biography because although much of the book was written by Preston Sturges himself, the book was finished by his wife, after his untimely and far too early death.

Sturges was a successful film director (his movies and original screenplays included 'Sullivan's Travels' and 'The Great McGinty') who had good times and bad patches. He made big money and lost it, made it again and lost it again. He was on the verge of a comeback when he had a heart attack and died, at the Algonquin Hotel in New York. He was 60-years-old.

'A good reason for writing one's autobiography is that it may prevent some jerk from writing one's biography. And this is all to the good, if only because what one writes oneself about persons and facts one knew first-hand will contain only such voluntary departures from the truth as one considers necessary to prevent a few husbands from shooting their wives, for instance (or vice versa), as opposed to the mountains of false statements, misspelled names, wrong dates and incorrect loci the well-meaning biographer usually comes up with after tracking one down through the morgues of defunct newspapers, the old letters of some of ones friends, and the very unreliable memories of people who knew one slightly.'

When Sturges died he left behind an unfinished autobiography and the usual collection of diaries and letters. His widow, Sandy Sturges, edited the material and, I believe, gave us the book that her husband began but never quite finished writing.

Partly through genuine modesty and partly through a desire to be honest (however brutal) Sturges wrote that he had much to be modest about. 'Between flops, it is true, I have come up with an occasional hit but…my percentage has been lamentable'.

He was being unfairly hard on himself.

And maybe that was because as he worked on his autobiography he was going through one of his bad, professional stages. And he was well aware that time wasn't on his side.

'I know that my life, even in these disagreeably trying times, is complete, although I don't know exactly why,' he wrote at the end. 'A man of sixty, however healthy, makes me think of an air passenger waiting at the terminal, but one whose transportation has not yet been arranged. He doesn't know just when he's leaving.'

Twenty minutes after writing that, Preston Sturges was dead.

Emma Hamilton
Norah Lofts
First published 1978

This is, I confess, only the second book by Norah Lofts that I've read. I found her previous non-fiction book 'Domestic Life in England' illuminating and interesting but no more. Most of her books were novels based on and around English history and that, I confess, is a genre which has never much interested me. She was, however, extremely successful.

I was given this book as a present and I found it utterly captivating – not so much for the information about Emma Hamilton but for what I learned about Horatio Nelson, England's greatest naval hero and one of most noteworthy heroes of any kind.

Beautifully illustrated (with relevant illustrations, which is a bonus) 'Emma Hamilton' is a story not so much about the extraordinary life of a blacksmith's daughter, who was clearly as bright and as determined as she was beautiful and full of charisma and sex appeal, but about a love affair with England's great hero – a man remembered now with the most noticeable statue in England.

Emma Hamilton's story had a bitter ending. After Nelson died at Trafalgar, shot in the back by a sniper while he stood on his ship Victory, wearing his dress uniform and a chest full of medals, she was left in comparative poverty. She descended into alcoholism, desperate self-pity and squalor in the French coastal port of Calais. It is, perhaps, not all that much of a coincidence that another exile, Oscar Wilde ended up in France. Both were broke and in disgrace and both had run away from shame.

Unlike most of the other titles collected for my one hundred books, I've read 'Emma Hamilton' only once – mainly because I only received it a short while before starting this book. But it is the best historical biography I have read and since it was written by an enormously successful historical novelist that is really not surprising.

But enough about Me
Burt Reynolds
First published 2015

'I've always made fun of myself, and I don't stop now,' writes Burt Reynolds in an Author's Note at the beginning of what is, I think, the funniest show-business autobiography. (Harpo Marx's book 'Harpo Speaks' is funny in parts but it is the charm which makes Harpo's book so loveable.)

There is a fictional quote at the start of the book which sets the tone.

'A movie star runs into an old friend on Rodeo Drive. The friend can't get a word in edgeways as the star goes on and on about her glamorous life: the A list parties, the Bel-Air mansion, the Bentley convertible. After what seems like an eternity she finally takes a breath and says: 'But enough about me. How did you like my last picture?'

The book is special because of the sometimes brutal honesty but mainly because it is often hysterically funny. There are wonderful tales about the people Reynolds worked with – especially close friends Dom DeLuise and Johnny Carson.

There has probably never been a more gutsy star in modern times (in the early days of motion pictures, Buster Keaton not only did his own stunts but did stunts for other actors too) and there is a good deal of respect for stunt men. 'I loved doing stunts,' writes Reynolds. 'Now I'm paying the price. My body is a wreck.'

And how about this for gutsy: 'Over the years I've had death threats, too. I never went to the police about them. I just recognised that there were lots of crazies out there and kept a pistol in my car.'

The secret of the book is that Reynolds never takes himself too seriously and there is never any self-pity. He's never a diva, always looking for the fun in any situation.

'I've had to reinvent myself four or five times,' he writes with inevitable honesty.

Reynolds turned down a lot of great films – including 'The Godfather', 'Die Hard', 'Pretty Woman', 'One Flew over the Cuckoo's Nest', 'Terms of Endearment', 'Star Wars', 'Witness' and 'James Bond'.

But he made a lot of great films too. And he was, I think, the first star to give us outtakes at the end of his films.

And he left us a great book. He even jokes about the awful hair. 'My hair will probably outlive everyone,' he says at the end.

The Day the Music Died
Larry Lehmer
First published 1997

Most people know that Don McLean's classic song 'American Pie' is about February 3rd 1959 – the day the music died. It was the day that Buddy Holly, Ritchie Valens and J.P.Richardson (aka the Big Bopper) were killed when the small plane in which they were travelling crashed.

Lehmer's book is meticulously researched, and sometimes seems detached, like a 272 page newspaper report, but that is because he has packed the book with quotes from everyone involved. The love shines through like a lighthouse beacon through a sea mist.

Most people probably remember the names Buddy Holly and Ritchie Valens and think of the Big Bopper as an afterthought. Certainly there have been more films and books about Holly and Valens than there have about Richardson.

But at the time of the crash, the Big Bopper was arguably the biggest name. It was certainly his name which gathered the headlines at the time, largely because of the huge success of his record 'Chantilly Lace'.

And I suspect that if they had all lived it would have been Richardson who would have become the greatest of the three legends. He wrote a mass of great songs, including, to my surprise 'Running Bear', sung by Johnny Preston. He also wrote 'Purple People Eater' and 'White Lightning' among many others.

'The Day the Music Died is, inevitably, a sad, tragic book full of 'what might have been' thoughts, but it is a great piece of music history.

Aubrey's Brief Lives
Edited by Oliver Lawson Dick

First published 1949

John Aubrey worked in the 17th century and wrote mini biographies of 426 people. The word 'brief', by the way, refers not to the longevity of the individuals concerned but, rather, to the length of Aubrey's biographies which vary from two words to 23,000 words.

Aubrey's biographies are opinionated, subjective and not the sort of thing you'd be likely to find in a proper old-fashioned, printed encyclopaedia, but they are well documented and therefore quite unlike their modern equivalents on the utterly unreliable and intrinsically corrupt pseudo encyclopaedias which exist on the internet. (I regard Wikipedia, for example, as entirely untrustworthy. Some editors will, for a fee, amend an individual's entry as required. Some biographical entries are believed to be written by editors wishing to demonise the subject for personal, professional or political reasons.)

Mr Dick's selection is taken from 50 volumes of Aubrey's work in the Bodleian Library at Oxford and from 16 volumes in a variety of other libraries. As a source book for those interested in social history, Aubrey's collection is more important than Samuel Pepys' diary.

Once he had decided on an individual to write about, Aubrey jotted down everything he could remember about them, including their appearance, their friends, their sayings and their published work. Dates and other facts were added later.

We can learn a good deal from these biographies. For example, this quote comes from a biography of William Butler, a physician who was born in 1535 and died in 1618 and whose patients included Henry, Prince of Wales.

'A Gent. With a red, ugly pumpled face came to him for a cure. Said the doctor, I must hang you. So presently he had a device made ready to hang him from a Beame in the roome, and when he was e'en almost dead, he cut the veines that fed those pumples and let out the black ugley Bloud, and cured him.'

Sometimes, Aubrey is not above some gossip.

Here he is on another of his lesser known subjects, Thomas Sutton. He was a lusty, healthy, handsome fellowe and there was a rich Brewer that brewed to the Navy etc who was ancient and he had married a young, buxom wife, who enjoyed the embraces of this more able performer as to that point. The old brewer doted on his desirable wife and dies and left her all his Estate, which was Great'.

The subjects of Aubrey's biographies included Francis Bacon, Robert Boyle, Jean Baptiste Colbert, Rene Descartes, William Harvey, Thomas Hobbes, Ben Jonson, John Milton, Thomas More, William Petty, Walter Raleigh, William Shakespeare, Philip Sidney and Edmund Spenser.

This is, perhaps, the most perfect book to take to a desert island.

The Missing Will: An Autobiography
Michael Wharton
First published 1984

Michael Wharton (who was born Michael Nathan) was a journalist. He was also one of the funniest writers ever to have existed. He created the 'Way of the World' column which was written under the name Peter Simple for the 'Daily Telegraph'. Collections of the columns were published and can still be found. They are gold nuggets in newspaper history.

'The Missing Will' is the first volume of Wharton's autobiography. The second volume is called 'A Dubious Codicil'. Both are worthy of inclusion in this collection but since I made a rule that no author could be included more than once, I'll cheat a little and include both books as a single entry.

The only annoying thing about Wharton's book is the fact that when I was preparing this entry I started re-re-reading it, got carried away and couldn't put it down.

Wharton was a contributor to the 'New Statesman', preferred Hitler to Stalin and hoped for Franco's victory in Spain. He loathed progress and technology. He changed his name to Wharton (his mother's name) from Nathan to escape, he said, 'from the oddity and even absurdity of my early life'. He wrote short pieces of fantasy for Punch magazine under the pseudonym Simon Crabtree. During the Second World War he was described as 'too passive and lacks initiative' but reported that 'these negative qualities …helped me to become an officer.'

After the war, Wharton wrote just about anything for anyone with a cheque book, including, in 1949, a script for the BBC about electricity generation, ignoring the fact that he knew nothing whatsoever about electric power generation. He edited the Football Association Yearbook without knowing anything much about football. After doing a great deal of work for the BBC, he joined the Daily Telegraph and became Peter Simple – one of the greatest and most outrageous of all comic inventions.

The Making of the African Queen
Katharine Hepburn
First published 1987
The subtitle of this extraordinary book is: 'How I went to Africa with Bogart, Bacall and Huston and Almost Lost My Mind.' (Lauren Bacall wasn't in the movie. She was there to keep Bogie company.)

Thirty years after making 'The African Queen', Katherine Hepburn felt the need (for whatever reason) to write a book about the experience. And thank heavens she did. It is surely one of the most wonderful, charming, revealing and fascinating books about a movie in particular, and the movies in general, that has ever been written.

Beautifully illustrated, beautifully written, beautifully witty and full of gorgeous anecdotes this is a book that is well worth hunting down. Hepburn is loving and kind and protective of Bogart (she doesn't tell us that a stunt man's torso was used for the awful scene with the leeches) and making the film was, she says, 'great fun'.

And she doesn't say that she was brave, but she was.

If you've seen the film you will know that much of it was made on location in Africa.

To avoid problems with the drinking water, the producers had taken a huge amount of what they thought was fresh water with them. Unfortunately, the water was contaminated and Ms Hepburn spent much of the film running to and from the loo. Bogart and Huston were untroubled, however. They didn't drink the water. They drank whisky. A lot of whisky.

An Innkeeper's Diary
John Fothergill
First published 1931

To describe John Fothergill as an innkeeper is like describing Samuel Pepys as a civil servant.

Fothergill was surely the real life original for Basil Fawlty (the hotelier played by John Cleese in the television series 'Fawlty Towers') and his diaries (there are several, thank heavens) are compelling, hilarious and sometimes dancing round the edge of unbelievable.

'In 1922,' writes Fothergill, 'I found that I must do something for a living, so I was compelled to take an Inn. Here, at least, I thought I might still be myself and give to others something of what I had acquired.'

He variously describes himself as a martyr and as high handed. He has little patience with fools and a fondness and respect for undergraduates, academics and the aristocracy.

Two women, whom he describes as 'shabby country style' asked for sandwiches and suggested egg or ham. Fothergill serves lamb sandwiches. The women complain, announcing that they are vegetarians and were unhappy at having to eat beef sandwiches. 'It was lamb,' Fothergill explains. The women argue, insisting it was beef. Fothergill offers to bring in the cook and the butcher's bill. 'You should know that I am obstinate,' warns one of the women. 'Then they should have been donkey sandwiches,' says Fothergill.

These days Fothergill wouldn't last a minute. He'd be destroyed on social media and the one star reviews would finish his business. What a pity.

Still, we have his diaries, which are a constant joy and a glorious memory of another time.

Pyrenean
J.B.Morton
First published 1938

J.B. Morton (his full name was John Cameron Andrieu Bingham Michael Morton) is mostly remembered as the original 'Beachcomber' of the 'Daily Express'. As 'Beachcomber', Morton wrote a slightly bizarre column about a parallel universe. 'Beachcomber' was to the 'Daily Express' what Peter Simple was, rather later, to the 'Daily Telegraph'.

'Pyrenean' is Morton's allegedly fictional story of a trek by 'Miles Walker' through the Pyrenees. Walker is, I rather suspect, Morton himself and this quiet adventure story of a man rediscovering a gentler, simpler, healthier life isn't a pilgrimage in the style of Hilaire Belloc's 'Path to Rome' (also a glorious book) but more a roaming in the style of the loveable escapist novels which Victor Canning and Francs Brett Young wrote about men running away from the exhausting tedium of responsibility.

At the end of his peregrinations, Morton (or rather Walker) enters a house where he buys 'the wine that Don Quixote drank' and 'drank a great deal of it so that it might mingle with my blood and fortify me against the cares of the world'.

'As I ate a meal that night in Guethary,' he writes, 'stuffing myself for dear life, a priest passing my chair said: 'Young man, you ought to take more exercise.'

You can take the Morton out of the humourist but, in the end, you can't take the humourist out of the Morton.

I never knew Morton but I'd bet this is the book of his of which he was proudest.

Morton went into a decline after his wife died (they'd been together for 47 years) and lived on bread and jam. (It is reported that he couldn't even boil an egg). In his fading years, he called every woman he met 'Mary', which was the name of the wife he missed so much.

The Boy who shot down an Airship
Michael Green
First published 1988
If you've never read any of Michael Green's books you have a treat in store. Green was best known for his 'Coarse' series of books. ('The Art of Coarse Rugby', 'The Art of Coarse Acting', 'The Art of Coarse Golf' and so on) and for politically incorrect and hysterically funny books such as 'Squire Haggard's Journal' and 'Tonight Josephine'.

The two volumes of Green's autobiography (this one and 'Nobody Hurt in Small Earthquake') are less well known but they are, without a doubt, the two funniest volumes of autobiography ever written. They may well be the two funniest books ever written.

In 'The boy who shot down an airship', Green discusses his adventures during the Second World War. They are the most wonderfully crazy war memoirs ever written.

Green couldn't write a dull line if he tried and his easy style captivates the reader. This is how an autobiography should be written. Here is Green working as a teacher in the British Army. 'Since I invariably went to sleep drunk and fully dressed all I had to do was to get up, light a fag and start teaching.'

The second volume describes his adventures as a junior reporter working for a local newspaper. If there is anything ever published that is funnier than` incredibly funny', this is it.

But, these two books aren't just funny; there is an added quality of nostalgia which makes them valuable both to those who can remember the middle years of the 20th century and to those who cannot. The world was very different then and anyone who believes in the virtues of progress should read these two books and reconsider their position.

Civil Disobedience
Henry David Thoreau
First published 1849
I felt guilty about including this book because everyone has read Thoreau's 'Walden' and 'Civil Disobedience' is often tacked on at the end of 'Walden' because it is considered too thin to be published as a book by itself, so the chances are that most people are already aware of it. But I wonder how many have read it. And since this is a book about books that might have slipped through the reader's radar here it is. (There is little point in including the Bible, Pilgrim's Progress etc., in a personal and eclectic guide to reading and I'd put 'Walden' into that august category.)

'Civil Disobedience' is the bible for all would-be revolutionaries, freedom fighters and social critics. I have read it, re-read it and quoted from it many times.

Here, as samples, are a couple of quotes (taken pretty well at random):

'It is not desirable to cultivate a respect for the law, so much as for the right. The only obligation which I have the right to assume, is to do at any time what I think right.'

'Law never made men a whit more just; and, by means of their respect for it, even the well-disposed are daily made the agents of injustice.'

I love Thoreau's philosophy of life. And I love this book.

The Dictionary of Accepted Ideas
Gustave Flaubert
First published 1954
It is surprising, but true, that although 'The Dictionary of Accepted Ideas' was created in the mid 19th century, it wasn't published as an independent work in English until a century later.

Flaubert's aims were to castigate clichés, misinformation and prejudice. While working on it he suggested that a suitable subtitle might be the 'Encyclopaedia of Human Stupidity'. It's sharp, it's funny and it seems to get increasingly apt as the years go by. It has spawned a thousand (inevitably inferior imitations).

Here are some examples:

Absinthe: Extra-violent poison: one glass and you're dead. Newspapermen drink it as they write their copy. Has killed more soldiers than the Bedouin.

Achilles: Add 'fleet of foot': people will think you've read Homer.

Actresses: The ruin of young men of good family. Are fearfully lascivious; engage in nameless orgies, run through fortunes; end in the poorhouse.

America: Famous examples of injustice: Columbus discovered it and it is named after Amerigo Vespucci. If it weren't for the discovery of America, we should not be suffering from syphilis and phylloxera.

Androcles: Mention him and his lion when someone speaks of animal tamers.

Apartment (bachelor's): Always in a mess, with feminine garments strewn about. Stale cigarette smoke. A search would reveal amazing things.

Archimedes: On hearing his name shout 'Eureka!' Or else: 'Give me a fulcrum and I will move the world'. There is also Archimedes' screw but you are not expected to know what it is.

Aristocracy: Despise and envy it.

Astronomy: Delightful science. Of use only to sailors. In speaking of it, make fun of astrology.

Authors: One should 'know a few'. Never mind their names.

The Smoking Diaries
Simon Gray
First published 2004

Gray wrote eight volumes of his memoirs and four volumes of what he called his 'smoking diaries' and, as so often seems to be the case, they are his best work. Maybe it is the raw honesty and the spontaneity which so often make diaries and memories so much better than a writer's other work.

This book is called a diary but you won't find a day or a date anywhere. The books in the series are, quite simply, magnificently despairing, angry and ruthless. They are rants. They are also very, very, very funny. Gray writes about his life, his smoking, his lung cancer and the overture to his death from cancer with a passion for a life and a devil may care ruthlessness for the virtue signalling, self-righteous numpties who rule our lives with puritanical zeal.

Simon Gray was, in case you don't know his name, a playwright and novelist. But it is these diaries for which he will be remembered after the bronze statues of much lesser men have disappeared – either through erosion or by being thrown into a canal.

Poetry in Motion
Tony Brooks
First published 2012

I have been a motor racing fan since I was a boy, when racing drivers were men of adventure who smoked a cigarette and drank a glass of wine during pit stops. Mike Hawthorn, my particular favourite when I was a boy, drove a Ferrari in a leather jacket with his bowtie fluttering in the wind at 150 mph. Drivers who wore overalls wore them in white without advertising. The cars looked like proper racing cars in red, green, blue or silver and there were no commercial logos or advertisements.

The drivers were heroic; genuinely facing death every time they went out onto the circuit. They were gentlemen, comrades in a war against the clock and the chequered flag.

Tony Brooks was a dental student, revising for his exams, when he was invited to drive a Connaught racing car at the Syracuse Grand Prix in Sicily. Can you imagine that happening now? He had been racing at weekends in a friend's Formula Two car and he'd been noticed. From dental school to Formula One in the time it takes to tell the story.

When he arrived in Italy, alone, Brooks found that the team had been delayed. So he rented a Vespa scooter and drove round the circuit to see what it looked like. When the team arrived, he climbed into a Formula One car for the first time in his life and, the first time he drove in anger, he qualified on pole. The next day he fought a long battle with the Maserati team and beat everyone. It was the first all-British victory since Henry Seagrave had won at San Sebastian in 1924.

'Poetry in Motion' describes Brooks' driving style – a unique combination of speed and something else. 'If I was going to have a team,' said Sir Stirling Moss, 'I would put Tony Brooks at number one, with Jim Clark alongside him. Tony was that good. He was careful with the car and very, very fast.'

I've selected 'Poetry in Motion' from all my books on motor racing because it is, quite simple, the best. It is truthful, modest, complete, dramatic, engaging, accurate, personal and readable. And the wonderful photographs provide an extraordinary record of motor racing in the 1950s.

A Better Class of Person
John Osborne
First published 1981
John Osborne wrote two volumes of autobiography, and at the end of this one he notes that in his pocket diary for 1955 the entry for 4th May reads: 'Began writing Look Back in Anger'.

'Look Back in Anger' was, of course, the play which changed his life and which changed the theatre (for a while at least). The relationship between Jimmy Porter and Alison (the play's protagonists) was modelled on Osborne's marriage to Pamela Lane, the first of Osborne's five wives.

'A Better Class of Person' is full of gossip and anecdotes and you just know it's all true. Here, for example, is a story about Richard Burton:

'Wales is the well-guarded reserve of its natural and principal species, the amateur. Someone suggested that Burton be invited to lead a National Welsh Theatre. A distinguished leader of the principality asked what were Burton's qualifications. It was explained that he had played Henry V at Stratford and a Hamlet at the Old Vic applauded by Churchill. The reply, which evoked no surprise, was, 'Yes, I see that. But what has he done in Wales.'

The second volume of Osborne's autobiography appeared ten years later, in 1991.

Both volumes are classics, both very readable, and both probably better than anything else he ever wrote. (How often this happens – particularly with playwrights.)

The Peep Show
Walter Wilkinson
First published 1927

A good many of my favourite non-fiction books describe life as it was before I was born, but with the honesty derived from the author's personal experiences, rather than being the academic views of a writer relying on second-hand experiences. Many of the books in this category are long since out of print, and when copies are available they are usually hard-bound library books, long ago tossed out without respect or ceremony to make room for the rows of DVDs from which the libraries can make some money.

Walter Wilkinson, who was born in 1888 and died in 1970, was a puppet man. More specifically he was a wandering Punch and Judy man. He made his own puppets, he made the costumes and he made a collapsible theatre with a wooden framework, a painted proscenium and striped curtains. He set off planning to travel round the country, pushing his theatre on two perambulator wheels and carrying light weight camping equipment. His simple aim was to set up his show in the towns and villages he visited, and to 'live simply on the pennies I collected by performing'. 'To me a book like 'The Peep Show' reveals England better than twenty novels written by clever young ladies and gentlemen,' wrote D.H.Lawrence.

'The Peep Show' is mainly the story of Walter Wilkinson's journey through North Devon, visiting Lynton and Lynmouth, Combe Martin, Barnstaple, Woolacombe, Saunton, Bideford and Westward Ho!. After Devon he travels to the Cotswolds. (There are many novels about men escaping from tedium and responsibility, and exchanging comfort and routine for adventure on the English roads. As I mentioned earlier, the best are the excellent 'escape' novels by Francis Brett Young and Victor Canning. I enjoyed reading them so much that I wrote one myself called 'Second Chance'. But D.H.Lawrence was right – the real thing cannot be beaten.)

Mr Wilkinson tells us everything we need to know. He describes the places he visits, the people he meets, the children he entertains, his perilous finances and the inevitable problems ('You can't stop here!') he has to overcome.

At the end of the book I challenge you not to envy his independence, his freedom and his adventures.

When I first bought 'The Peep Show' there were no internet bookshops. For years I hunted around the shelves of second-hand bookshops, looking for copies of Mr Wilkinson's other books. (A couple were promoted inside The Peep Show).

Having rediscovered The Peep Show for this book I realised I might be able to find other volumes of his adventures through the internet. Within a day I had bought every one of his seven other books published between 1927 and 1948. Serendipity.

A Moveable Feast
Ernest Hemingway
First published 1964
During the 1920s, Paris was full of Americans and especially full of Americans who wanted to be writers. There can hardly have been any writers left in America. The strength of the dollar against the

French franc meant that even a relatively unsuccessful, impoverished writer could live well enough, living in hotels and eating and drinking and cafes in bars.

How much of this book is true and how much is fanciful is something of a mystery but, apart from allowing for a little poetic licence here and there I have no doubt that most of the book is as accurate as any volume of autobiography ever is.

The people you would expect to read about are all there. Sylvia Beach, the proprietor of the legendary bookshop 'Shakespeare and Co', and the long-suffering publisher of Ulysses by James Joyce. Scott and Zelda Fitzgerald are there, with Scott drinking too much and being rude (especially to anyone he considered his inferior, which was most people). Zelda, his wife, has her first breakdown.

Hemingway writes and rewrites 'The Sun Also Rises' (published in England as 'Fiesta'). He runs out of money. There is always a strong whiff of tragedy in the air. There is much gambling, horseracing and drinking. Six day bicycle races. Lost manuscripts. Ford Madox Ford. Ezra Pound. Gertrude Stein. Picasso. Hemingway's first wife Hadley. Oysters and the magic of Paris in the 1920s.

The first sentence sums up the book: 'But this is how Paris was in the early days when we were very poor and very happy.'

The critics won't agree but I think this is Hemingway's best and most personal book. It's the only book of his that I've read more than twice.

Studies on Malaria
Sir Donald Ross
First published 1928

Sir Donald Ross was a doctor who, in 1902, was awarded the Nobel Prize for medicine. He was given the prize for his work on the transmission of malaria.

I found my first edition copy of this book (Ross's invaluable personal account of his work) in the withdrawn bin at the Royal Society of Medicine in London when I was still a Fellow. (I was later invited to resign after complaints from drug companies over the fact that one of my publishers, Pan paperbacks, had mentioned my

Fellowship of the RSM in the biography of a book of mine.). Oddly, and obviously coincidentally, the complaints occurred as I was having one of my regular disagreements with the pharmaceutical industry.

It seemed to me strange that the RSM Library should dump a book by one of Britain's foremost medical scientists, but I have often found valuable and informative books available on the 'withdrawn' shelf of public libraries too.

Ross's book seems especially valuable to me for his personal observations. For example, in 1902 (the year he was awarded the Nobel Prize) Ross was receiving a salary of £300 a year plus a small pension. In today's money that would give him about £40,000, since the British pound has lost over 99% of its value since 1902. He was unhappy about this because the School of Tropical Medicine in Liverpool, where he was working, was receiving donations of £2,500 a year 'chiefly due to my work'. Pointing out that he was not 'a sanitary knight-errant', Ross threatened to resign and take up a consulting practice in London. He then received a letter from Lord Lister offering him his own laboratory, an assistant and £500 a year.

The lives of great men can be just as fraught with frustration and disappointment, and financial shortcomings, as everyone else's.

Rural Rides
William Cobbett
First published 1830
We all need heroes for they give us direction and purpose, and enable us to believe that the world is not entirely populated by the sort of small-minded, self-obsessed time-servers we see parading their vanity and ignorance on television, or representing us in Parliament. Or, indeed, sitting behind the counter at the Post Office or behind a desk at the Tax Office.

'Rural Rides' first appeared in instalments in Cobbett's own publication called 'Political Register', and first appeared in a book in 1830 – again published by Cobbett himself. (Independent publishing has a long, proud history.)

Cobbett was a journalist, author, politician and campaigner and he wrote (and published) around 30 million words. He collected and published Parliamentary debates and found time to run a farm.

Between 1821 and 1826, Cobbett wandered around the English countryside, recording what he saw and heard. He saw how life was changing and he championed farm labourers who lived in dire circumstances, always on the edge of starvation.

'Rural Rides' is a magnificent book and as valuable a description of England in the early 19th century as anything we have. Cobbett looks at anything and everything. He wrote about the treatment he tries for the 'hooping-cough' and he describes how the soil changes from one part of England to another. And he's always brave and brutally honest. 'Deal is a most villainous place. It is full of filthy looking people.' He attends a sale, meets a turkey farmer who started his business after reading Cobbett's book 'Cottage Economy', and describes how a labourer who would, in 1771, have been paid 13 shillings 1 penny a week was in 1826 paid just eight shillings a week. Cobbett cared passionately for people and this is an immensely sympathetic and readable book.

Cobbett was as great a hero as England ever saw. He was 72 when he died and by then he had contributed more to England and to mankind than any politician in history. If you want to know more there is an essay about Cobbett, and several other authors mentioned in this book, in my book 'The 100 Greatest Englishmen and Englishwomen'.

Understanding Media
Marshall McLuhan
First published 1964

I bought my copy of 'Understanding Media' when it first came out and I was still at school. It has survived in my library through a great many clear-outs.

Over the years I have given umpteen thousands of books to charity shops. On many occasions I have filled the car with cardboard boxes full of books I needed to give away. I regret all those 'lost' books, many of which I have subsequently bought again, for a second or a third time.

But 'Understanding Media' has survived every clear out for over half a century.

I cannot remember whether or not I guessed when I bought 'Understanding Media' that I was going to spend much of my life working as a writer, or if I just bought it, as I bought so many books, because I was hoovering up knowledge – especially knowledge that wasn't part of the school curriculum.

'Understanding Media' may be rather old now, and some of it may seem dated, but the principles remain the same. McLuhan's first chapter is entitled 'The medium is the Message' and that was surely a phrase that became part of the English language. The concept is crucial. His second chapter is entitled 'Media hot and cold'.

It was, I think, that second chapter which had the greatest impact on me. McLuhan describes television as a cool medium and radio as a hot medium.

Here's how McLuhan defined the two.

'There is a basic principle that distinguishes a hot medium like radio from a cool one like the telephone or a hot medium like the movie from a cool one like the television. A hot medium is one that extends one single sense in 'high definition'. 'High definition is the state of being well filled with data. A photograph is, usually, 'high definition. A cartoon is 'low definition' simply because very little visual definition is provided. Telephone is a cool medium, or one of low definition, because the ear is given a meagre amount of information. On the other hand, hot media, do not leave so much to be filled in or completed by the audience.'

Even at 18 I realised that this meant that the way a presenter worked on television had to be very different to the way they worked on the radio.

The book made McLuhan famous and much sought after as a speaker. I remember reading that soon after the book's publication, McLuhan received an invitation to speak at a meeting organised by a large American company. When he said 'No thank you' the organiser assumed he was negotiating for a higher fee and upped the money being offered. McLuhan hadn't been negotiating. He simply didn't want to give the speech. Eventually the offered fee rose to an absurd sum and McLuhan could no longer say No. The result was that his popularity as a speaker rose dramatically, and his new fee became his standard fee.

(Much the same thing happened to Benny Hill, the TV entertainer. American television companies were determined to entice him to work in America but Mr Hill didn't want to go and had plenty of money for his simple lifestyle. The sums on offer became astronomical but he never went. The Americans who had been offering the huge fees couldn't understand it.)

McLuhan predicted the existence of the World Wide Web (or something like it) around 30 years before it appeared. In a book called 'The Gutenberg Galaxy' (published in 1962) McLuhan wrote: 'The world has become a computer, an electronic brain…And as our senses have gone outside us…we shall at once move into a phase of panic terrors, exactly befitting a small world of tribal drums, total interdependence…Terror is the normal state of any oral society, for in it everything affects everything all the time.'

McLuhan also predicted that advances in electronic media would create what he called a 'global village'. And he didn't think it would work out well. 'When people get close together, they get more and more savage and impatient with each other.'

Much later, P.J.O'Rourke pointed out that: 'With social media, we've done something worse than create a world where we can hear what everybody says. We've created a world where we can hear what everybody thinks.'

And that, of course, would be fine if everybody who shares their thoughts had a brain to think with.

A Short History of the World
H.G.Wells
First published 1922

When I was small I was enormously impressed by H.G.Wells's 'A Short History of the World'. It is still an enormously impressive achievement, a great tour de force and a superb starting point for the non-historian, though I realise, sadly, that it attracts sneers from modern historians who regard it as old-fashioned and therefore inevitably racist and sexist in tone.

Wells' book was written to be read as a novel (which is not surprising when you consider his other books include such classics as 'The History of Mr Polly', 'Kipps', 'The Time Machine', 'The Invisible Man' and 'The War of the Worlds') and is a shorter version of his book 'Outline of History'. Wells wrote the book as an introduction to history but I have no doubt that for many it became the first course, the second course and the third course too.

The book starts at the beginning of time and was revised by Wells up until his death in 1946 to deal with the events of the Second World War. There is a chapter headed 'The Present Outlook' and another, the final chapter, entitled 'Mind at the End of its Tether'.

At the back of the book there is an excellent chronological table – a quick guide which takes us up to the surrender of the Germans at the end of World War II and the death of American president Roosevelt.

The Lessons of History
Will and Ariel Durant
First published 1968

'The lessons of History' is much heavier going than H.G.Wells' book 'A Short History of the World – though it is still accessible even for a non-historian like me. In comparison with Wells, the Durant's style is fairly academic and a trifle pompous at times.

The book begins with this: 'As his studies come to a close, the historian faces the challenge: Of what use have your studies been?' And continues with these questions: 'Have you learned more about human nature than the man in the street can learn without so much as opening a book? Have you derived from history any illumination of our present condition, any guidance for our judgements and policies, any guard against the rebuffs of surprise or the vicissitudes of change?' (You now see what I mean about their style.)

The Durants ask a good many questions.

'Have we really outgrown intolerance, or merely transferred it from religious to national, ideological or racial hostilities?'

'Are our manners better than before, or worse?'

'Have our laws offered the criminal too much protection against society and the state?'

'Has there been any progress at all in philosophy since Confucius?'

'Are we ready to scuttle the science that has so diminished superstition, obscurantism and religious intolerance, or the technology that has spread food, home ownership, comfort, education and leisure beyond any precedent?'

They leave us to provide the answers.

The Durants were (in the 1960s) alert enough to understand that progress isn't all that we might like to think it is. And alert enough to know that progress is an unstoppable force.

'We have laudably bettered the conditions of life for skilled working men and the middle class, but we have allowed our cities to fester with dark ghettos and slimy slums.'

Indeed, so.

This isn't a book to read on the beach on a sunny day. It's a book that triggers contemplation – possibly more suitable for perusing while sitting in front of a blazing log fire in late November.

And it is none the worse for that.

Will Durant is the author of another excellent little book entitled 'The Greatest Minds and Ideas of All Time.'

The Devil's Dictionary
Ambrose Bierce
First published 1906

Like other books in my list, 'The Devil's Dictionary' began life as a newspaper column. Bierce started it in 1881 and added to it, as the fancy took him, until 1906 when it was published as a book under the title 'The Cynic's Word Book'. Bierce didn't much like the title, which appears to have been thrust upon him.

'The Devil's Dictionary' is much more appropriate and is, I would think, much closer to Bierce's taste. The book consists of many entries, some quite short, some quite long and some in verse form. There are some terrible puns.

'Here are a few sample entries:

'Harbor: A place where ships taking shelter from storms are exposed to the fury of the customs.'

'Hand: A singular instrument worn at the end of the human arm and commonly thrust into somebody's pocket'.

'Harangue: A speech by an opponent, who is known as an harangue-outang.'

'Hatred: A sentiment appropriate to the occasion of another's superiority.'

'Vote: The instrument and symbol of a freeman's power to make a fool of himself and a wreck of his country.'

'Wheat: A cereal from which a tolerably good whisky can with some difficulty be made, and which is also used for bread. The French are said to eat more bread per capita of population than any other people, which is natural, for only they know how to make the stuff palatable.'

'Wine: Fermented grape-juice known to the Women's Christian Union as 'liquor', sometimes as 'rum'. Wine, madam, is God's next best gift to man.'

Born in Ohio, U.S, Bierce was a journalist and the author of brilliant, sardonic short stories. At the age of 71 he mysteriously disappeared in Mexico. No one has any idea what happened to him.

Tao Te Ching
Lao Tzu
First published 4th century BC
Although Lao Tzu, who was an older contemporary of Confucius, has been enormously influential on Chinese thinking (the book is sometimes known by the author's name, by the way) his work seems to come in and out of fashion.

Lao Tzu was a philosopher and a poet and his book can be read as either or as both. He was the founder of Taoism. Inevitably, some scholars claim that the book was written by many authors. (They do the same with other historical figures – such as Hippocrates.) I prefer to stick with the idea of a single author.

Here are some of my favourite entries:
'Without stirring abroad,
One can now see the whole world;
Without looking out of the window
One can see the way of heaven
The further one goes
The less one knows
Therefore the sage knows without having to stir
Identifies without having to see
Accomplishes without having to act.'
And

'The people are hungry
It is because those in authority eat up too much in taxes
That the people are hungry
The people are difficult to govern
It is because those in authority are too fond of action
That the people are difficult to govern.'

The Paris Sketch Book
Mr Titmarsh (William Makepeace Thackeray)
First published 1840

I have three copies of this book. The reason is simple. We once had three homes (I refuse to apologise for what seems like an extravagance since we bought them ourselves out of taxed income and they served different purposes) and I liked to keep a copy of each of my favourite books in each library. And, although we now have just one home, I have never thrown out the extra copies of this book.

'The Paris Sketch Book' was originally written as a number of essays and articles under the pseudonym Mr Titmarsh, before being published in book form in 1840. Some sources give a different publication date but Thackeray himself dated the first edition as 1840 and even if he was wrong I prefer to go with him. Some editions have illustrations (which are excellent) by Thackeray himself.

Today, of course, reviewers and critics complain that the book is old-fashioned, jingoistic and snobbish (which is rather ironic since Thackeray invented the word 'snob' for use in his excellent volume 'The Book of Snobs'.)

The reviewers and critics miss the point, of course, since the book is supposed to be funny and racist and it consists of sketches which were written in Paris, rather than specifically about the city. (I had a similar experience with a humorous book of mine called 'Secrets of Paris'. Bizarrely, some reviewers criticised the book, which contains a number of light-hearted pieces about the French capital, because it contains nothing about the Louvre and no lists of hotels or train times.)

There are some mentions of Paris in Thackeray's book and they still ring true. Here he is at Versailles: 'The town is, certainly, the most moral of towns. You pass, from the railway station, through a long, lonely suburb with dusty rows of stunted trees on either side and some few miserable beggars, idle boys and ragged old women under them.'

Tourists who arrive in Versailles by charabanc would, of course, miss all this.

Thackeray's description of Versailles as it was in its heyday, and was when he was there, is marvellously evocative and acidic for, like Twain and Dickens he was a brilliant writer and a brilliant writer who travels can produce a better travel book than a traveller who chooses to write a book.

Seven Pillars of Wisdom
T.E.Lawrence
First published 1926

Winston Churchill described this book as ranking with the greatest books ever written in the English language. 'As a narrative of war and adventure it is unsurpassable,' he wrote.

'Seven Pillars of Wisdom' (of which I have a very lovely early edition) was originally self-published and was a financial disaster for Lawrence who lost money on every book which he sold.

Indeed, the book was something of a trial for the author.

It is, I think, now well known that Lawrence lost the briefcase containing a first draft of the book when he was changing trains at Reading station. Appeals for the manuscript to be returned met with silence and so Lawrence had to rewrite the whole book. The fact that he had destroyed all his notes when he'd finished the first version of the book made the task infinitely more difficult. Astonishingly, he produced 400,000 words (in longhand) in just three months.

Lawrence has always been a great hero of mine and I have copies of all of his books. 'The Mint', which has the by-line '352087 A/c Ross' on the cover, tells the story of Lawrence's time in the Royal Air Force, where he lived under the name Ross to try to escape his extraordinary fame. (After this pseudonym was exposed, Lawrence joined the Royal Tank Corps under the name T.E.Shaw.)

It has, of course, become fashionable for critics to attack

Lawrence. It seems sad, to say the least, that the British, or at least some of them, always feel that they must attack our national heroes – especially if they are perceived as English. (Lawrence was actually born in Wales but his parents, who weren't married, moved to England when he was a boy.)

I really don't think this happens in any other country.

The Case Books of Dr John Snow
John Snow (edited by Richard H.Ellis)
First published 1994

Dr John Snow was almost certainly the most influential of all British physicians and one of the most significant in world history. Snow made two huge contributions to medical practice.

First, he introduced anaesthesia into medical practice, and, in particular, for women in confinement. Second, by removing the handle from the Broad Street pump in Soho he helped prevent the spread of cholera in London.

I managed to obtain a complete copy of John Snow's personal casebooks which include, in amazing detail, his daily medical work from 17th July 1848 until March 5th 1858 (just under three months before his death at the age of 45) and they make extraordinary reading.

In 2003, a poll organised by a magazine for hospital doctors voted Snow 'the greatest doctor of all time'. Quite right too, though I wonder how many of today's medical students, nurses and other health care workers have even heard of him.

Dr Snow kept meticulous case books in which he recorded his daily visits and consultations but until 1994, the case books (consisting of 200,000 words) remained unpublished and available therefore only to a very select group of doctors.

In 1994, the 'Wellcome Institute for the History of Medicine' published a single edition of the three volumes, which had been edited for publication by Richard H.Ellis.

The book contains every word of the journals, which ran from 1845 to 1858.

Nothing else I have ever read provides such a detailed account of medical practice at that time as this volume, which also provides an invaluable insight into the work of the man who has been voted 'the greatest doctor of all time'.

The Pleasure of Finding Things out
Richard P Feynman
First published 1999
I first discovered Richard Feynman when I read his memoir 'Surely You're Joking Mr Feynman' which was published in 1985.

This book is an excellent introduction to Feynman and his varied work. It includes a wonderfully entertaining essay about his experiences as a safe cracker and an excoriating account of a report to the Space Shuttle Challenger enquiry.

Feynman was a brilliant theoretical physicist who worked at the Los Alamos Scientific Laboratory during the Second World War. After the War he became Professor of Theoretical Physics at Cornell University, worked on quantum electrodynamics and shared the Nobel Prize in 1965. He was not, however, just a brilliant scientist (though that would be enough for most people). He was also a wonderful lecturer and writer (who could explain the most complex problems in the simplest way), an iconoclast, an eccentric and a man with great passions.

He was, quite possibly, the only Nobel Prize winner to have been a dedicated and accomplished bongo player.

Helio-Tropes
John Parmenter
First published 1625
I don't have an original, first edition copy of this and I rather doubt if you'll be lucky enough to find one. My copy is a 1904 edition edited by Perceval Landon.

I have many unusual, not to say sometimes strange, books in my library but I have to confess that this is probably the strangest.

John Parmenter was probably a priest and nothing much is known of him except for the fact that he was a biblical scholar and that he left us this short book of inscriptions (or 'posies') written for sundials.

The inscriptions are accompanied by short descriptions.

Here are some examples of Parmenter's collected 'posies':

'I sleep at sunset and I work at Dawn. Tis onlie Idlers come upon this Lawne.

'As you watch my shadow moving, Past each minute's ordered grooving, God's almighty purpose proving, Rest is nearer, nearer as you look.

'If I am wrong, 'tis your fault or 'tis God's'

'The moon makes silly work of both of us'

'Not least among thy many duties, Sun.

It amuses me greatly to think of a man spending a good chunk of his life collecting sundial descriptions. I only wish Mr Parmenter had explained where each one had been found. It would have been an entertaining adventure to retrace his footsteps.

I cannot remember where I found this book but I fancy it may have come in a boxful of assorted second-hand books. I used to buy boxes of first editions and assorted rare books from a London auction house which specialised in books. The auctioneer used to sell books in batches if they were difficult to categorise individually. Sorting through the contents of huge boxes of books was a great joy for Antoinette and me.

Sailing Alone around the World
Joshua Slocum
First published 1900
If a team of editors were looked in a room for a week they wouldn't be able to think up a better title for Captain Slocum's book than the one it has.

In April 1895, Captain Slocum set off round the world – by himself – and travelled 46,000 miles. He sailed in a 36 foot wooden sloop called simply 'Spray' and he had such extraordinary adventures that it is difficult to believe the account isn't fictional. He made no attempt to sail round the world without stopping, by the way. This wasn't a race.

But the book isn't fiction. It definitely isn't fiction. It is the most extraordinary account of one man's lonely adventure.

First published as a serial in the 'Century Illustrated Monthly Magazine', between September 1899 and March 1900, Slocum's story is just as astonishing as that of Daniel Defoe's fictional Robinson Crusoe (which was based on the real life adventures of Alexander Salkirk who spent four years and four months as a castaway on an uninhabited island in the South Pacific.)

Slocum paid for his journey by sending articles to the Boston Globe newspaper, by trading in salvaged tallow, by charging visitors to look around the 'Spray' and by collecting and selling exotic shells. He also gave lectures at the various ports where he stopped – just as Mark Twain had done on his world tour.

On his way round the world, Slocum encountered pirates off Gibraltar, met Henry Stanley in Africa and dealt with savage Indians in Tierra del Fuego. He survived tempests and coral reefs and lived for much of his trip on the fish he caught.

'Sailing Alone around the World' is a treat in store for anyone who hasn't yet discovered it. It's perhaps, one of those books to read while sitting in a comfortable chair, beside a roaring log fire with a plateful of toasted and buttered crumpets and a cup of tea beside you.

The Outsider
Colin Wilson
First published 1956
When it was first published, 'The Outsider' made Colin Wilson a literary superstar overnight.

Wilson famously wrote the book in the British Museum, sleeping on Hampstead Heath to save money. After publication, one critic wrote: 'Not since Lord Byron woke up one morning and found himself famous, has an English writer met with such spontaneous and universal acclaim.'

The Daily Mail (which was a newspaper back in the 1950s) described the book as having been given 'the most rapturous reception of any book since the War'. Time magazine described it as a 'brilliant and unusual analysis'. And the New Statesman said that reading it was 'a necessary stage in the development of any honest contemporary thinker'.

It seems strange and sad that both the book and its author are now pretty much forgotten, and subject to the usual online sneers. Wilson himself wrote that after a month of gaudy success (he was compared to Plato, Shelley and Shaw) the roundabout came to a halt and began to revolve in the opposite direction. Wilson was attacked viciously and with malice aforethought, though it is difficult to discern any reason other than jealousy and a reaction against his success.

'The Outsider' is a book of philosophy and literary criticism. It is an analysis of the artistic and psychological problems which we all face. And it is a book in which Wilson explains that men of genius are outsiders who reject the everyday world and seek out another world – a world of ideas and of the spirit. Wilson himself said later that the foundation stone of all his thinking was the recognition that man's moments of freedom tend to come under crisis or challenge, and that when things are going well, man tends to allow his grip on life to slacken.

Re-reading 'The Outsider' for this book (for the third time), I did find that Wilson seems sometimes obtuse and sometimes rather pompous. And I fear that he is guilty of overthinking. There aren't many laughs in the book either. But the book is well worth its place on my list.

Peking to Paris
Luigi Barzini
First published 1907

I adore this book. I once lent my copy to a friend and after I (eventually) got it back, swore that it would never leave my library again.

'Peking to Paris' is an account of a car race which was run in 1907 and which Luigi Barzini Senior won in the horseless carriage belonging to Prince Borghese.

It was, without a doubt, the most utterly insane motor race of all time. Illustrated with scarcely believable photographs, 'Peking to Paris' is a charming and utterly extraordinary account of something that happened over a century ago but which describes a world we can now hardly recognise.

Barzini tells how the journey was completed in 60 days, with the race being won by nearly three weeks. The car was a slightly modified Itala. The engine and chassis were standard but the springs and wheels were stronger than usual.

Prince Borghese and his chauffeur sat in the front with Barzini in the back. A special petrol tank held 150 litres of fuel – sufficient for 1,000 kilometres. The Prince had as sponsors the Russo-Chinese Bank (hoping to promote trade between Europe and the Far East) and the Nobel company which owned nearly all the Siberian oil wells and wanted to promote the petroleum industry and to encourage other motorists to use plenty of fuel.

The book is full of surprises and awe-inspiring moments.

Determined to win the race, Borghese at one point commissioned local craftsmen to build a wooden wheel as a necessary replacement. At another crisis point, a raft had to be built to cross a river. Villagers were recruited en masse when it was necessary to pull or push the car out of mud. There were no roads over much of the journey and at one point the car was driven along the tracks of the Trans-Continental Railway – with the occupants quietly hoping that no train would come.

I bought my copy in a second-hand book store in London's Charing Cross Road in the 1970s. It is a treasure.

The Fifteen Decisive Battles of the World
Sir Edmund Creasy
First published 1851
My copy of this book is beautifully bound in blue leather with gold leaf decorations, though the corners and top of the spine are worn, as should be the case with a much loved and oft-consulted volume.

Creasy, who also wrote 'The Rise and Progress of the English Constitution' and who was a famous former Chief Justice of Ceylon (when it was called Ceylon and had not become Sri Lanka), selected his 15 battles because they had vital consequences both at the time and subsequently.

The 15 battles Creasy selected were:
The battle of Marathon (BC 490)
Defeat of the Athenians at Syracuse (BC413)
The battle of Arbela (BC 331)

The battle of the Metaurus (BC 207)
Victory of Arminius over the Roman legions (AD 9)
The battle of Chalons (AD 451)
The battle of Tours (AD 732)
The battle of Hastings (AD 1066)
Joan of Arc's Victory over the English (AD 1429)
Defeat of the Spanish Armada (1588)
The battle of Blenheim (AD 1704)
The battle of Pultowa (AD 1709)
Victory of the Americans over Burgoyne (AD 1777)
The battle of Valmy (AD 1792)
The battle of Waterloo (AD 1815)

I wonder if Creasy would add to his list if he were resurrected and allowed to add to his selected 15 battles. It is difficult to think of individual battles (as opposed to wars) which were as significant as the ones he chose.

The Social Contract
Jean-Jacques Rousseau
First published 1762

'The Social Contract' is about moral responsibilities, freedom, relationships and civilisation. Surprisingly, for such an important book, it is quite a short volume

Rousseau believed that laws should be just but realised that all practical systems of law can be seen to be unjust. He believed that to be free we have to put ourselves under rules devised by honest, good, law-givers. He believed it was a bad thing to have a master but a good thing to have a tutor. He had no patience with hypocrisy and proposed a death penalty for those whose conduct was at variance with the religious principles they proclaimed. He argued that no agreement that enslaved one party could be valid because any agreement which is wholly to the advantage of one party and wholly to the disadvantage of the other must be void in natural laws.

Rousseau's concept of a republic bears no relationship to what we have now: totalitarian states where the people are controlled by government edict, secret police, party rule and brain washing. Rousseau would regard what we have now as despotism – to be roundly condemned.

Rousseau understood that a man's private interests and preferences might be very different to his public responsibilities, and that a man's yearning for independence might encourage him to regard his contributions to the common cause as painful. The greatest potential paradox of his philosophy is that men must be free within the constraints of society.

Rousseau was persecuted and exiled and like Philippus Aureolus Theophrastus Bombastus von Hohenheim (aka Paracelsus – and one of my medical heroes) and spent the last years of his life a victim of ignorance, prejudice and intolerance, constantly searching for a peaceful retreat.

The Art of War
Sun Tzu
First published 1905

'The Art of War' was, of course, written much longer ago than 1905. It was, indeed, written two and a half thousand years ago in the 5th century BC. But, amazingly, it wasn't until 1905 that an English translation first became available. It is of interest that this surprisingly short book has been available in Russian for centuries and has been the bible of strategy and tactics in China since it first appeared.

For almost two decades, Sun Tzu was a general for the King of Wu. During that time the King never lost a battle. But after Sun Tzu died his recommendations were forgotten, the armies of Wu were defeated and the kingdom became extinct.

'In peace prepare for war, in war prepare for peace,' wrote Sun Tzu. 'The art of war is of vital importance to the State. It is a matter of life and death. A road either to safety or ruin.'

James Clavell argued that if our military and political leaders had studied the 'Art of War', America would not have lost the Korean War; the Vietnam War would have been very different, The Bay of Pigs fiasco would not have happened, the British Empire would still exist and, in all probability, neither World War I nor World War II would have taken place. Businessmen and businesswomen of all kinds have reported that they have found Sun Tzu's advice invaluable.

So, what are the secrets of the Art of War?

Well, here are three titbits which I marked when I first read it:

'If your opponent is of choleric temper, seek to irritate him. Pretend to be weak, that he may grow arrogant.'

'The general who wins a battle makes many calculations in his temple ere the battle is fought.'

'He who wishes to fight must first count the cost.'

The Natural History of Selborne
Gilbert White
First published 1789

I almost didn't include the Reverend White's masterpiece on the grounds that it is too well known. But, although that may have been the case I am not sure that White's masterpiece of observation is in as many homes as it used to be. And it is one of the Great Books of all time.

The book is written as a series of letters, addressed to Thomas Pennant and the Hon. Daines Barrington, and in an 'advertisement' included in my edition the Rev White suggests that 'if stationary men would pay some attention to the districts in which they reside, and would publish their thoughts respecting the objects that surround them, from such materials might be drawn the most complete county-histories, which are still wanting in some parts of this kingdom'.

White writes beautifully about anything and everything around him from thunderstorms to cats. Here he is describing how different creatures open hazelnut shells:

'There are three creatures, the squirrel, the field-mouse, and the bird called the nut-hatch which live much on hazle nuts; and yet they open them each in a different way. The first, after rasping off the small end, splits the shell in two with his long fore-teeth, as man does with his knife; the second nibbles a hole with his teeth, so regular as if drilled with a wimble, and yet so small that one would wonder how the kernel can be extracted through it; while the last picks an irregular racked hole with its bill: but as this artist has no paws to hold the nut firm while he pierces it, like an adroit workman, he fixes it, as it were, in a vice, in some cleft of a tree, or in some crevice; when, standing over it, he perforates the stubborn shell. We have often placed nuts in the chink of a gate-post where nut-hatches have been known to haunt, and have always found that those birds have readily penetrated them. While at work they make a rapping noise that may be heard at a considerable distance.'

In his very first letter, the Rev White explains the position of Selborne (the extreme eastern corner of the county of Hampshire) the type of soil, the local streams, the style and depth of local wells (which, he reported, produced a fine, limpid water, soft to the taste and much commended by those who drink the pure element but which does not lather well with soap).

He tells us that a local spring called Well-head, produced, after a hot summer and a preceding dry spring and winter, nine gallons of water a minute.

He reports that some local oaks have furnished much naval timber but that the trees on the freestone grow large but are 'what workmen call shakey, and so brittle as often to fall to pieces in sawing'.

He describes the activities of the hedgehogs in his gardens and fields and reports that young hedgehogs are born blind. 'No doubt their spines are soft and flexible at the time of their birth, or else the poor dam would have had but a bad time of it in the critical moment of parturition, but it is plain that they soon harden'.

He describes everything in his village with precision and quiet affection. 'When brown owls hoot, their throats swell as big as a hen's egg. I have known an owl of this species live a full year without any water. Perhaps the case may be the same with all birds of prey.'

It is, in my estimation, the most complete, most perfect book on natural history ever written. The world would be considerably poorer and less knowledgeable without 'The Natural History of Selborne'.

The Road to Serfdom
F.A.Hayek
First published 1944
A note on the frontispiece tells me that I first started to read this book on a plane from Heathrow to Nice in 1996. I have absolutely

no idea why I was flying to Nice or what I did when I got there other than finish Hayek's masterpiece.

'The Road to Serfdom' is about the problem of finding, and preserving freedom, in a planned society.

Writing in the early 1940s, Hayek warned that our liberty would disappear if governments (or any other groups) attempted to direct all economic activity according to a single plan, laying down all society's resources should be directed to serve particular, definite ends.'

My copy of the book contains more marks, under-linings and comments than any other book I own. And I found this quote: 'We were the first to assert that the more complicated the forms of civilisation, the more restricted the freedom of the individual must become.'

The quote comes, as a warning, from a certain B.Mussolini.

And here is Hayek on the perils of socialism: 'Although we had been warned by some of the greatest political thinks of the 19th century, by de Tocqueville and Lord Acton, that socialism means slavery, we have steadily moved in the direction of socialism. And now that we have seen a new form of slavery arise before our eyes, we have so completely forgotten the warning, that it scarcely occurs to us that the two things may be connected.'

And Hayek reminds us that: 'Mr Hilaire Belloc, in 'The Servile State' (1913) explained that 'the effect of socialist doctrine on capitalist society is to produce a third thing different from either of its two begetters – to wit, the Servile State.' (Belloc's book is, of course, also well worth reading and is included in this book.)

Down and Out in Paris and London
George Orwell
First published 1933
After he left Eton, Eric Blair (who wrote as George Orwell) worked in Burma, in the Indian Imperial Police (it will, perhaps, be something of a surprise to some to know that George Orwell was once a policeman). After Burma, Blair moved to Paris and this book is largely an account of his time in the French capital where he worked as a plongeur (a dishwasher) in a large, elegant hotel.

'I think one should start by saying that a plongeur is one of the slaves of the modern world,' wrote Orwell. 'Not that there is any need to whine over him, for he is better off than many manual workers, but still, he is no freer than if he were bought and sold. His work is servile and without art; he is paid just enough to keep him alive; his only holiday is the sack. He is cut off from marriage, or, if he marries, his wife must work too. Except by a lucky chance, he has no escape from this life, save into prison. At this moment there are men with university degrees scrubbing dishes in Paris for ten or fifteen hours a day.'

Later, Orwell concludes that the plongeur's slavery is more or less useless. 'For, after all, where is the real need of big hotels and smart restaurants?' They are supposed to provide luxury, but in reality they provide only a cheap, shoddy imitation of it. Nearly everyone hates hotels.'

And thus, slowly, day by day, dirty dish by dirty dish, line by line, was born arguably the most powerful fiction writer of the 20th century – George Orwell.

England have my Bones
T.H.White
First published 1936

I'm a huge fan of T.H.White's work. His fairy tale 'The Once and Future King' was a major classic the minute he put the last full stop in place. His love story to a bird of prey 'The Goshawk', touched my heart when I first read it, and still touches it even though I know I should disapprove.

All White's books are wonderful.

'England have my Bones' is a prose poem to England and the English countryside, written by someone whose life was full of passion. He writes about learning to fly, about trees, about horses, about shooting, about fishing, about snakes and about why only one hat is of any use at all – the deerstalker.

P.G.Wodehouse invented a world for Bertram Wilberforce Wooster, Jeeves, the young men of the Drones' Club and a battalion of aunts, but it now seems almost equally impossible to believe that White's world existed. It existed, nevertheless, just as surely as it now just a memory.

In some ways White was a guest in the world where he lived. 'As my income dwindles,' he wrote, 'I shall give up shooting first of all, then hunting, then flying, then fishing.' He drove a Bentley which I suspect he couldn't possibly afford.

Here is an entry from the 18th of May 1934:

'But it is worthwhile to live with a little bit of danger. One is so surrounded in peace time with the depravity of the modern world. If for my whole life I were to redeliver the same lectures, nag at the same people, prattle the same scandal, what else would there be for it except to take earnestly to drink? One would forget the foulness of the world and give oneself an illusion of happiness at any rate. Even sitting in the same chair rots one's soul. Decent men ought to break all their furniture every six months. Failing that, they ought to fly. The objective of an uncomfortable or perilous life is the enjoyment of comfort and safety in between.'

I can forgive White anything and everything for he wrote beautifully.

But I'm keeping my favourite chair. And I shall never fly again for the process has become intolerable.

Duveen
S.H.Behrman
First published 1953

To say that Duveen was an art dealer is like saying that Shakespeare wrote plays, Dickens wrote novels and Winston Churchill was a politician. Duveen was 'the' art dealer.

This book by Berhman first appeared as a series of articles in the New Yorker magazine in 1951. (It is extraordinary, is it not, how many wonderful books began life as a series of articles in a newspaper or magazine.)

Duveen's success was built upon a single observation – that there were a lot of people in Europe who had plenty of art but no money and a lot of people in America who had plenty of money but no art to put on their walls or boast about.

Duveen made it his life's work to correct the imbalance.

He started buying art in Europe at the age of 17 and he never stopped travelling to America to sell what he had bought. He had galleries in London, Paris and New York and he travelled constantly between the three.

Art experts regarded Duveen with sometimes ill-disguised but more usually well-hidden contempt. They thought he knew little about the pictures he was selling. The rich Americans who bought from him thought he knew more about art than anyone alive or dead.

But, whatever anyone thought about him, Duveen invariably won – steadily pushing up prices so fast and so effectively that it was only when he died that the market collapsed.

Behrman's book is full of wonderful anecdotes.

I like this human touch.

'When Duveen's daughter was a very little girl the family went to Dieppe for a holiday. Duveen took the child to the beach. She dipped her foot in the sea and found the water too cold, so she wouldn't go in. Duveen collected some sticks and borrowed a tea kettle, built a fire on the beach, heated some water till it steamed and poured it into the sea. His daughter then went in without a whimper.'

The Life of John Mytton
Nimrod (Charles James Apperley)
First published 1837

History is full of eccentrics. Philip V of Spain used to fish for carp in a bucket of fish. Sir Humphry Davy, who discovered the anaesthetic effects of nitrous oxide, worked on early batteries and invented the safety lamp, is reputed to have wandered around dressed like a Dutch pirate with porpoise-hide hip waders spattered in salmon blood, and Ludwig Wittgenstein, the philosopher, allegedly subsisted entirely on cornflakes, arguing that once you've found a diet which agrees with you, it makes sense to stick with it. John L Sullivan, the champion boxer, would drink a whole bottle of cognac during a fight.

England has always bred more eccentrics than any other country and the Earl of Rochester, for example, is one of the best known.

Today, many (or more probably most) of those described as eccentric should more accurately be described as exhibitionists. Their eccentricities are planned, devised and marketed as publicity gimmicks. Television and tabloid newspapers have created thousands of ditch-water celebrities who constantly dream up new ways to promote themselves.

But John Mytton, known to his friends as 'Mad Jack', was the greatest of all genuine English eccentrics. He had no book, film or TV show to promote. He wasn't selling himself to anyone. He lived from 1796 to 1834 but crammed a good deal of eccentricity into a very short life and sat, quite simply, on that rather dangerous line between eccentricity and madness. All other eccentrics must be measured against him though he was simply described by his family as 'high spirited'.

As a boy, Mytton was asked to leave Westminster School after a year for 'fighting with the masters'. He then went to Harrow where he lasted three days. When it was decided that he should attend Cambridge University, he arranged for 2,000 bottles of port to be ready for his arrival. In the end he changed his mind and didn't go to Cambridge. There is no record of what happened to the port. When his creditors became a little too aggressive, Mytton moved to France. In a hotel in Calais he developed hiccups and decided to get rid of the problem by giving himself a fright. He set fire to his nightshirt. This cured the hiccups but he was badly burned. Advised to stay in bed for a month he arranged to go out for dinner that evening. But when his dining companion sent a two horse equipage for him, Mytton, covered in bandages, refused to get into it, claiming that he would sooner walk than ride in a carriage with less than four horses. He walked a mile and a half to dinner.

On his 21st birthday, Mytton inherited £60,000 and valuable estates. He was, therefore, hugely rich. However, in the remaining 17 years of his life he got through more than £500,000 and ended up bankrupt.

In 1819, Mytton decided to seek election as MP for Shrewsbury. While campaigning he walked round the constituency with £10 notes pinned to his hat. As the notes were taken so they were replaced. Mytton spent £10,000 in this way and won the election by 384 votes to 287. When Mytton got to the House of Commons he found the first debate he attended to be 'uninteresting'. He left and never went back.

Every morning Mytton drank five bottles of port before lunch. If the port ran out (not something that happened often) he would drink eau-de-Cologne or lavender water.

Mytton liked to drive his gig into rabbit holes at high speed to see if it would turn over. (It invariably did.) When a passenger complained that his carriage driving was reckless and might overturn the carriage, Mytton scoffed and said: 'What? Never been upset in a gig? What a damned slow fellow you must have been all your life. He then deliberately ran the carriage up a steep incline and overturned it so that the passenger could experience an 'upset'.

He kept 60 cats which he dressed in liveries suitable to their breeds. He was even fonder of dogs and had 2,000 of those. When his favourite dog Tizer was losing a fight with a friend's dog, Mytton bit the other dog's nose and held on until the dog gave in.

Mytton was fond of practical jokes. On one occasion he rode into his dining room in full hunting costume. To the alarm of his guests he was riding his pet brown bear called Nell at the time. Mytton frequently took his favourite horse into the house, sat it by the fire and served it mulled port. He once replaced the last few pages of the local vicar's sermon with pages from the 'Sporting Magazine'. On another occasion he got his horse dealer drunk and put him to bed with two bull terriers and Nell, the brown bear. Mytton sent the same horse dealer to a banker in Shrewsbury, ostensibly to collect money for him. He gave the dealer a note to hand to the banker, who was also a governor of the local mental hospital. The note read: 'Sir, please admit the bearer, George Underhill, to the lunatic asylum. Your obedient servant, John Mytton'.

On separate occasions, Mytton fought both dogs and bears armed with nothing more than his teeth. In winter he went duck hunting in his night shirt or, on occasion, completely naked. He invented a game which involved chasing rats across a frozen pond while wearing skates.

Although he started life a rich man, Mytton got through money very quickly. His wardrobe contained 700 pairs of boots, 150 pairs of riding breeches, 1,000 hats and nearly 3,000 shirts.

After being released from debtor's prison in 1832, Mytton met an attractive young woman on Westminster Bridge. He asked her where she was going. She said she didn't know. Mytton offered her £500 a year to live with him. She accepted and spent the last two years of his life with him in Calais.

Mytton was just 38-years-old when he died, in prison, from

alcohol poisoning. More than 3,000 friends and acquaintances attended his funeral.

If Mytton's life story entertains you, then I would also recommend the book 'Squire Walton' by Gilbert Phelps.

Charles Walton, of Walton Hall, Near Wakefield was unusual to say the least. He was an explorer and a writer and he believed in blood-letting so much that as an old man he reported that he had it done to him 160 times. He celebrated his 82nd birthday by climbing barefoot to the top of an oak tree. And at the age of 83 he dissected a rancid gorilla in his dining room, after he'd finished his evening meal. As you do.

A Narrow Street
Elliot Paul
First published 1942

For 18 years an American newspaperman called Elliot Paul (who was co-founder of a famous magazine called 'Transition') lived in a street in Paris called Rue de la Huchette. The street is close to the Seine and Notre Dame and it is narrow and now on the tourist route from Saint Germain to the area opposite Notre Dame. I suspect most visitors to Paris will have walked down it.

'A Narrow Street' is not about the street itself but about the people who lived in it – including an old woman who one day decided to give her legs a rest. She retired to bed for the rest of her life. (When I was GP I had a patient, an Irishman, who made the same decision except that once a year he climbed out of bed, got dressed, summoned a taxi, travelled to the airport and flew to Ireland to watch the hurling championships. He then came home and went back to bed for the next 51 weeks. He was looked after by a number of female neighbours who did his shopping, cooking, washing and ironing for him.)

There is in Paul's book a man who stuffs animals, a tramp who sleeps on the pavement, a hotelier, a carpenter, an incompetent accordion player, a couple of conspirators, a little girl, a grocer, a female cook who liked bawdy songs and a postman and a milkman.

Mr Paul writes about them and the city itself with care, honesty affection and some frustrations. It is one of the very best books written about the French capital.

Oddly enough, the blurb on the back of the 1947 Penguin edition tells us that Elliot Paul wrote two books about Paris; this one and one called 'The Last Time I Saw Paris'. I have them both and they're actually largely the same book with different titles, though 'The Last Time I Saw Paris' contains a piece about Elliot Paul's time in Ibiza.

Shakespeare and Company
Sylvia Beach
First published 1956

Born in 1887 in New Jersey, U.S.A., Sylvia Beach ended up living in Paris where she opened a bookshop called Shakespeare and Company. The bookshop is still there, now the most famous English language bookshop on continental Europe and a honey trap for Parisians, expatriates and tourists. I have, over the decades, bought dozens of books there, many of them second-hand and many stamped with the famous Shakespeare and Company rubber stamp.

Miss Beach was (like her compatriot and fellow expatriate Gertrude Stein) a lesbian. She lived openly with Adrienne Monnier, another bookseller, to whom her autobiography is dedicated.

Shakespeare and Company was founded in Paris because Ms Beach couldn't afford to open a bookshop in New York. The first version was situated in the rue Dupuytren. Sylvia sent her mother a cable saying: 'Opening bookshop in Paris. Please send money.' Mrs Beach sent her daughter every penny she had.

(A bookshop with the same name was opened by George Whitman in the rue de la Bucherie, in sight of Notre Dame. The shop was badly damaged by fire and many enormously valuable first editions were destroyed. It was rebuilt and, at the time of writing, still exists.)

Sylvia Beach's shop was soon popular with writers, and Sylvia became good friends with Scott Fitzgerald, Ernest Hemingway, Ezra Pound, Robert McAlmon, Ford Madox Ford, T.S.Eliot, Gertrude Stein, Andre Gide, Janet Flanner and an Irishman called James Joyce who couldn't find a publisher for a book he'd written called Ulysses.

'Would you let Shakespeare and Company have the honour of bringing out your Ulysses?' said Beach to Joyce one day. She had no publishing experience but in 1922 she published it. He was the only author she ever published.

It was a wonderful day when I managed to buy a copy of her original edition at auction.

The Selective Ego
James Agate
First published 1976

In his day, James Agate was London's most influential theatre critic. He wrote vividly and with an enthusiasm which made him wildly popular, about actors such as Lawrence Olivier, John Gielgud and Peggy Ashcroft. Because of his power, he knew everyone in the world of theatre and in the broad acres around it. He could be nice and he could be horrid but he was never, I suspect, accused of being ordinary.

But it is not for his reviews that Agate is remembered – those are now largely forgotten, as is the way with most criticism.

Agate kept a diary between 1932 and 1947 and he did so knowing (or at least hoping) that it would one day keep him. The nine published volumes of those diaries are a treasure trove of anecdotes, gossip (often scurrilous) and information but they are not (weren't) easy to find. Even with the aid of the internet it took me several years to collect them all.

'The Selective Ego', published in 1976, is a collection of excerpts from all nine books and it should be read as a taster for the real thing – all of which I heartily recommend.

Agate loved golf, Hackney ponies, young boys and life – though not necessarily in that order. If he had been alive in the 21st century he would have been reviled and imprisoned and his diaries would have been withdrawn from publication (though there is nothing remotely offensive in them).

Life other writers of that period (such as Beverly Nichols) Agate was homosexual and lucky to avoid the courts for that alone. He had trouble enough with the taxman and although he was very well paid he was perpetually broke and was at one point sent to prison because he owed twenty pounds.

Wind, Sand and Stars
Antoine de Saint-Exupery
First published 1939
Best known today for his book 'The Little Prince', Antoine de Saint-Exupery was a pioneer pilot in commercial aviation. In 1944 he and his aeroplane disappeared over the Mediterranean while returning from a reconnaissance mission. There is still much mystery about precisely what happened and there are still some who believe that the pilot committed suicide. Towards the end of 'Wind, Sand and Stars' the reader finds this short paragraph: 'Comrades of the air! I call upon you to bear me witness. When have we felt ourselves happy men?'

'Wind, Sand and Stars' is de Saint-Exupery's account of his years as a commercial pilot. (He was, incidentally, the Comte de Saint-Exupery.)

He enrolled as a student pilot in 1926 and was employed to fly between Toulouse in South Western France and Dakar in French West Africa.

'We lived in fear of the mountains of Spain over which we had yet to fly, and in awe of our elders,' wrote de Saint-Exupery.

The book is about friendship, flying, crashing and surviving in the desert.

Three crews are down in the desert, and here is what Saint-Exupery writes:

'Altogether, there were about ten of us, pilots and mechanics, when we made ready for the night. We unloaded five or six wooden cases of merchandise out of the hold, emptied them and set them about in a circle. At the deep end of each case, as in a sentry-box, we set a lighted candle, its flame poorly sheltered from the wind. So, in the heart of the desert, on the naked rind of the planet, in an isolation like that of the beginnings of the world, we built a village of men.'

And a page or so later he writes:

'Each man must look to himself to teach him the meaning of life. It is not something discovered: it is something moulded. These prison walls that this age of trade has built up round us, we can break down. We can still run free, call to our comrades, and marvel to hear once more, in response to our call, the pathetic chant of the human voice.'

There is, by the way, a bust in his memory in a small park in the 7th arrondissement, close to Les Invalides, in Paris. Few men are more deserving of a statue in their memory.

I see from the stamp inside the book that I bought my copy from 'Shakespeare and Company' in Paris.

Life worth Living
C.B.Fry
First published 1939

To say that C.B.Fry was the greatest sportsmen who ever lived (or ever will live) is not an exaggeration (as you might suspect) but an understatement.

Fry was a proud Englishman ('…my ancestors did not come over with William the Conquerer. They were here to meet him when he landed', he writes on the first page) and a consummate natural sportsman.

Fry played cricket and football for England and played (for Southampton) in an FA Cup Final. He played rugby for Oxford University and held the world long jump record.

In addition to his athletic achievements, he was a Captain in the Navy and wrote a number of books. He worked as one of the first radio commentators and was a regular panellist on radio programmes such as Any Questions and the Brains Trust.

If I try to list his achievements I'll be depressed for a week. In his seventies he was still fit enough to be able to jump backwards, from a crouching position, onto a mantelpiece.

The Albanian people were so impressed by the numerous activities, skills and talents of this English superman that they asked him to be their King. They probably fancied a monarch who could jump backwards onto a mantelpiece. It would have certainly put him head and shoulders above monarchs who simply waved and simpered. Fry declined, presumably because he couldn't fit it into his schedule.

Oh, and he also edited an incredibly successful magazine (the CB Fry magazine) which was stuffed with amazing stories.

'Life Worth Living' by C.B.Fry is a magnificent introduction to the life of one of the most amazing men to have lived. Fry was a Corinthian, a gentleman and a genius at living. In his 80s he was still writing witty Latin verse and sharp, pertinent articles for The Cricketer magazine. I've read biographies of Fry but this, his autobiography, is brilliant.

'Life worth Living' is a joyful book, crammed with anecdotes about sport, publishing, the navy, travel and even Hollywood. The man was irrepressible and inexhaustible.

Hesketh Prichard: A Memoir
Eric Parker
First published 1924

Few are more entitled to be described as 'Renaissance Men' than Hesketh Prichard – a man now too rarely remembered but a real hero in the 'Boys' Own Paper' style.

Hesketh Vernon Hesketh Prichard was born in India in 1876 and died in England in 1922, but in that woefully short life he packed more adventures and achievements than most who live twice as long. (I assume that his parents rather liked the name Hesketh since they gave it to him twice.)

It's difficult to know where to start.

As an explorer he travelled to Haiti, to the Panama Canal, to Norway and to Patagonia (and wrote a splendid book about his journey in Patagonia).

As a journalist he wrote for publications as varied as Country Life, Cornhill Magazine and the Daily Express. He wrote an illustrated paper for the Journal of the Royal Geographical Society.

He wrote a series of bestselling, hugely popular novels and wrote articles and stories with his mother.

He travelled incessantly and went to Canada to shoot Caribou. Curiously, despite his enthusiasm for hunting and shooting creatures, he was also a dedicated naturalist who, fought incessantly against the plumage trade.

A keen sportsman, Prichard played first class cricket (he was friends with Conan Doyle and W.G.Grace and other first class cricketers), appearing for Hampshire (he ended the 1902 season second in the country bowling averages) and in 1903, he represented the Gentlemen versus the Players at Lords and was a great success. In 1907, he captained an England cricket team visiting America where he was a hugely popular after dinner speaker.

Prichard's cricket career came to an end when the war began in 1914 and, as you might by now expect, he was a hugely successful soldier. Although he was rejected by both the Guards and the Black Watch regiments because of his age (he was 37) he was employed at the War Office and invented the modern version of sniping. In 1916, he founded the first Army sniping school. He wrote an excellent book on sniping (which is wonderfully illustrated), which is I am told still regarded as the classic book on the subject.

Prichard left us with a number of excellent books (including 'Sport in Wildest Britain'). And his play Don Q was so successful that he had to appear on stage in response to calls for 'Author! Author!' Tragically, by then he was so weak with the undiagnosed illness which killed him (possibly a form of blood poisoning) that he could hardly stand let alone walk. But he did walk and he stood long enough to tell the audience that the success of his play belonged to the producer and the actors rather than the author.

Hesketh Vernon Hesketh Prichard was a true gentleman as well as a hero.

One Day and Another
E.V.Lucas
First published 1909

E.V.Lucas's books are largely forgotten now, overtaken by time and forgotten by reprint publishers. It's a huge pity because his books, although old-fashioned, do not deserve to be abandoned.

Lucas was one of the greatest of all English essayists, sometimes serious, always knowledgeable and frequently witty.

He was, I suspect, one of the first English journalists to discover the fun of making up lists. Here, for example, is a list entitled 'Foibles of Literary Men' which appears in this book:

Keats liked red pepper on toast.
Dickens was fond of wearing jewellery.
Joaquin Miller nailed all his chairs to the wall.
Edgar Allan Poe was inordinately proud of his feet.

Robert Browning could not sit still. With the constant shuffling of his feet, holes were worn in the carpet.

Longfellow enjoyed walking only at sunrise or sunset and he said that his sublimest moods came over him at these times.

Hawthorne always washed his hands before reading a letter from his wife. He delighted in poring over old advertisements in the newspaper files.

Thackeray used to lift his hat whenever he passed the house where he wrote 'Vanity Fair'.

Darwin had no respect for books as books and would cut a big volume in two, for convenience in holding, or he would tear out the leaves he required for reference.

Oliver Wendell Holmes used to carry a horse-chestnut in one pocket and a potato in another to ward off rheumatism.

I have a large collection of books by E.V.Lucas, mostly his books of essays, picked up for pennies in second-hand book shops. Small hardbacks, they are invariably a convenient pocket size. I picked this book pretty well at random from my collection. I have yet to find a book of his which I did not thoroughly enjoy.

Publish and be damned
Hugh Cudlipp
First published 1953

Cudlipp's story of a newspaper (Britain's Daily Mirror) was written to celebrate the paper's 50th anniversary and it quickly became a classic account of the workings of what was then an enormously popular and powerful tabloid newspaper.

There are chapters about Zec, the paper's star cartoonist during World War II, William Connor (Cassandra) the acid inked columnist who was so badly wrong in his criticism of P.G.Wodehouse, and Godfrey Winn whose sugary articles about dogs and his mother delighted millions and nauseated millions more.

And Cudlipp deals honestly and in detail with the paper's proprietors and its relationship with Winston Churchill during the Second World War.

By the time he reached the end of his book, the Mirror had a circulation of over 4,500,000 and a readership of 11 million.

Under the masthead, the paper carried this promotional line: 'The biggest daily sale on earth'.

'Publish and be Damned' was a phenomenon when it was first published and the title became a well-known phrase or saying. Today the book is a valid historical document which explains how a newspaper can be designed to connect with its readers and still retain its integrity and independence.

I suspect that not many modern editors or publishers have read it. They might be more successful if they had done so.

Adventure Capitalist
Jim Rogers
First published 2003

Jim Rogers became a professional investor in 1968. He had 600 dollars. Twelve years later, at the age of 37, he retired with enough money for the rest of his life.

He had made his money as co-manager of an offshore hedge fund, largely exploiting untapped markets in little known areas of the world.

When he retired, Rogers decided that he wanted to see more of the countries where his investments had been so profitable. But he didn't want to go round the world from airport to airport or from the comfort of a cruise ship. He wanted to see the world in the raw.

And so in late 1990 he set out on a two year journey around the world; a trek that took him 100,000 miles and through dozens of countries. He made the trip on a motorcycle and the book he wrote about the trip was a bestseller entitled 'Investment Biker: Around the world with Jim Rogers'.

This book is the follow up and describes his adventures while driving round the world in a custom built yellow Mercedes. He travelled with his fiancée, the trip took them through 116 countries (including Angola, Colombia, East Timor and Sudan) and they drove through jungles, blizzards, deserts, epidemics and war zones. It was the ultimate rich man's adventure.

But it isn't just an adventure story. 'Adventure Capitalist' is also a valuable guide book for investors.

'If you learn nothing else in your life,' writes Rogers towards the end of the book, 'learn not to take your investment advice, or any other advice, from the US Government – or any government.'

A Cry from the Far Middle
P.J.O'Rourke
First published 2020

This was P.J.O'Rourke's 19th book and sadly it was his last. It is a book of essays on just about everything political and it is written in O'Rourke's trademark, inimitable, acerbic style. (Many years earlier, O'Rourke worked at the magazine 'National Lampoon' which ran a famous cover showing a picture of an adorable dog with a gun to its head. The caption was: 'If you don't buy this magazine we'll shoot this dog.' It is reputed that the magazine's sales doubled.)

The book includes a heartfelt rant against the Internet of Things ('your juicer is sending fake news to your Fitbit about what's in your refrigerator') and a suggestion that politicians should be licensed (a sentiment with which I wholeheartedly agree.)

O'Rourke points out that every other profession has some form of accreditation or certification but that although we license plumbers, estate agents, beauticians and barbers we do not licence politicians.

And he suggests that politicians should be tested before being given their licence.

'There would be an essay question: 'Say nothing of substance in 5,000 words or more. Extra credit for saying less at greater length.''

And of course there would be a section requiring politicians to define essential terms such as 'boodle', 'pork barrel', 'gerrymander', 'carpet bagging', 'graft' and 'gravy train'.

In a 'Pre-Preface' compiled after the world had changed at the start of 2020, O'Rourke wrote: 'Journalists are supposed to provide answers. But all I've got is questions. Starting with: 'isn't somebody supposed to be in charge?'

All 19 books by P.J.O'Rourke are worth reading.

The Prince
Machiavelli
First published 1640 (in English translation)

When I first read Machiavelli's 'The Prince' I was still at school, hoping to go to university to study medicine. In my copy of the book I marked this passage:

'When trouble is sensed well in advance it can easily be remedied; if you wait for it to show itself any medicine will be too late because the disease will have become incurable. As the doctors say of a wasting disease, to start with it is easy to cure but difficult to diagnose; after a time, unless it has been diagnosed and treated at the outset, it becomes easy to diagnose but difficult to cure. So it is in politics.'

And that, remember, was written in the 16th century by an Italian author who died in 1527.

'The Prince' is still the wisest book on political affairs and the bible for politicians and statesmen. When it was written, it was considered such a shocking book that its author was regarded as depraved and his book considered to be inspired by the Devil.

Machiavelli was a very early political advisor, a spin doctor, a man who worked on the edges of political life and who became a full-time author only after he was fired from public life.

Modern politicians should, perhaps, pay particular attention to the section headed: 'The need to avoid contempt and hatred'.

Brothel in Pimlico
Roy Brooks
First published 1985

When I was young I remember reading and enjoying the adverts which an estate agent called Roy Brooks used to insert in the Sunday Times.

The advertisements were unlike anything I had ever seen before and unlike any I've ever seen since. They were brutally, spectacularly, disarmingly, delightfully original. They were impudent and honest. They ran from 1950 to 1971.

Eventually a clever publisher collected some of the adverts and printed them in two volumes called 'Brothel in Pimlico' and 'Mud, Straw and Insults' (which was first published in 2004). The best examples from the two books were then collected and published, rather confusingly, as 'Brothel in Pimlico'.

So what was so special about these advertisements?

Here is an example for one of Brooks' house adverts, taken at random:

'Fashionable Chelsea, Lamont Rd. Do not be misled by the trim exterior of this modest Period Res. With its dirty broken windows; all is not well with the inside. The décor of the 9 rooms, some of which hangs inelegantly from the walls, is revolting. Not entirely devoid of plumbing, there is a pathetic kitchen and 1 cold tap. No bathrm., of course, but Chelsea has excellent public baths. Rain sadly drips through the ceiling on to the oilcloth. The pock-marked basement flr. indicates a thriving community of woodworm; otherwise there is not much wrong with the property. In the tiny back garden an Anderson shelter squats waiting…Lse 40 yrs? G.R.£50. SACRIFICE £6,750.'

The rest of the book of full of similar advertisements.

No modern estate agent would dare to publish such advertisements or, sadly, be allowed to do so. These are a memory of simpler times which were, sometimes, far more honest than life today – despite all the legislation and regulations which control our every move.

This is a daft book to include in this volume. It offers no great insights. But it's a very personal choice and it is here as a very small reminder of what freedom (and humour) we have lost.

The Journals of Arnold Bennett
Arnold Bennett
First published 1954

Arnold Bennett is rather unfashionable today but he wrote some wonderful novels (my favourites are The Card, The Grand Babylon Hotel and Riceyman Steps, rather than the better known 'Anna of the Five Towns' and 'The Old Wives' Tale') and he was the most influential and well-paid literary critic of his day.

Bennett's journals were originally published in four volumes covering the years 1896 to 1929 but in 1954 a selection from all those years was published in a single volume.

Bennett kept his journal from his youth until the end of his life. He wrote down each day's experiences and thoughts wherever he was – in London, Paris, Fontainebleau or Brighton. He kept the diary in hotels and on ships (from yachts to liners) and in Austria, Greece, Italy and the United States.

He wrote down details of his health, how many words he had written that day and how much money he had earned. By the time he died, his journals contained a million words. He described people he had met, detailed conversations he had shared and jotted down ideas for books He wrote about the books he was reading and the shops he patronised.

Bennett wrote beautiful novels but it isn't difficult to argue that his journals are his most magnificent masterpiece and his lasting achievement.

In Search of England
H.V.Morton
First published 1927

H.V.Morton was certainly the best travel writer of his generation but I'd go further and say he was (and still is) the best and most prolific, most consistent, most readable and most loved of all travel writers. He wrote countless books which were reprinted innumerable times. In the days when England was well supplied with second-hand book shops, Morton's books were invariably available by the dozen.

Morton's great skill was that he wrote as an ordinary tourist. He described the places he had visited, the cafes where he ate and the people he met. I have never found a pompous or boring sentence in any of his books. He never makes assumptions and is never patronising, though I have no doubt that there will be some today who, devoted as they are to taking offence, will find some reason to consider him politically incorrect.

In this book he describes how he visits Christchurch in Dorset and is lured into a café by a charming waitress standing in the doorway. She asks if he would like some tea. He says he would. She then asks if he'd like a lobster. It is 4.30 pm and this seems such a strange suggestion, almost indecent, that he says yes, he would like a lobster. He then says 'yes' to 'basins of Dorset cream, pots of jam, puffy cakes oozing sweetness, ramparts of buns and crisp rolls.'

'The only thing I missed at this tea party was the Mad Hatter,' he concludes.

He is a great listener, our Mr Morton, sometimes naïve (though possibly deliberately so), and by his own account always trusting and willing to be led.

His books are a joy. If you haven't discovered them then I recommend them highly. I have a shelf full of Mortons.

The Clumsiest People in Europe
Mrs Favell Lee Mortimer (edited by Todd Pruzan)
First published 2005

When I first obtained a copy of this I was suspicious that it might be one of those joke books written for the Christmas market. But it isn't. It's real and this is a selection (edited by Todd Pruzan) of the best (or worst) of books which were published in the middle of the 19th century by Mrs Favell Lee Mortimer.

Mrs Favell Lee Mortimer left England just twice but, on the basis of her rather limited travels, she managed to become an enormously successful author of books about the countries and people of the world. She wrote 16 books for children and became something of a literary superstar with her work selling millions of copies and being translated into 38 languages.

Mrs Favell Lee Mortimer (nee Bevan) was one of the daughters of a co-founder of Barclays bank and she married (unhappily) at the age of 39. She decided she had a mission to educate the world. Ignoring the fact that her own travels had taken her outside England just twice (once to Edinburgh and once to Paris and Brussels) she wrote freely and confidently about a world she'd never seen and people she'd never met.

Here are some of Mrs Mortimer's many gems:

'It would be well if the Germans were more neat and clean, especially the poor people.'

'The Turks are so grave that they look wise. But how can lazy people really be wise?'

'(The English) are not very pleasant in company, because they do not like strangers.'

'Though the Welsh are not very clean, they make their cottages look clean by white-washing them.'

'I think it would almost make you sick to go to church in Iceland.'

'The Burmese are very deceitful, and tell lies on every occasion.'

'One of the chief faults of the Scotch, is the love of whisky. Another fault is the love of money. They often ask more than they ought, and are very slow to give.'

To describe Mrs Mortimer as racist and xenophobic really isn't enough is it?

Clubland Heroes
Richard Usborne
First published 1953
None of the heroes described in Mr Usborne's book could possibly exist today and the authors would be banned, pilloried and quite possibly put into prison for daring to invent such men.

'Clubland Heroes' is about the characters created by John Buchan, Dornford Yates and Sapper. They are all strong, thoroughly masculine characters. And this is a book about a world in which men who were members of traditional London clubs fought (and beat) cads and spies. The cads and spies they defeated were mostly foreign, of course, often German, and the clubland heroes were brave, knowledgeable and independently rich. They drove wonderful motor cars (Rolls Royces and Bentleys were usual since both were, at the time English marques and therefore preferable to the sort of foreign machinery preferred by the villains), had chauffeurs and valets, were crack shots and excellent pugilists and regularly rescued maidens in distress. They lived either on their estates in the countryside or in elegant apartments in central London.

The heroes (who include Richard Hannay and Bulldog Drummond) were fantastic heroes for generations of boys, and when the cinema came along they moved to the silver screen with ease; with Alfred Hitchcock's 'The Thirty Nine' steps being the most successful example, though a number of films were made about Bulldog Drummond (and, in addition E.W.Hornung's creation Raffles). There are at least three other versions of 'The Thirty Nine Steps' – though none of them matches Hitchcock's version starring Robert Donat and Madeleine Carroll.

There was no sex, no worries about money and nothing improper. Policemen were generally polite and knew their place. But the heroes, although politically incorrect in every imaginable way, were always scrupulously decent, honest and brave. They were men who expected to read a freshly ironed Times newspaper with their breakfast kippers.

Such men don't exist anymore and I doubt if they ever did. Their world was created by their authors (in the same way that Wodehouse invented a world for Bertie Wooster and Jeeves) and they were the forerunners of James Bond, Quiller and other modern heroes.

Performing Flea
P.G.Wodehouse
First published 1953

There are, I suspect, more biographies and bibliographies of P.G.Wodehouse than of any other English author since Shakespeare. I have one huge bibliography which is impossible to lift with one hand.

But for anyone who wants to know more about P.G.Wodehouse (the most consistently funny writer to have ever laid a finger on a keyboard in earnest) there is nothing better available than this collection of letters from 'Plum' Wodehouse to his chum Bill Townend, who was himself a highly successful author.

The letters include valuable advice such as 'The more I write the more I am convinced that the only way to write a popular story is to split it up into scenes, and have as little stuff between the scenes as possible.'

And this: 'A villain ought to be a sort of malevolent force, not an intelligible person at all.'

Plum advises his friend that he 'must not take any risk of humanising your villain in a story of action'.

In a later letter, Plum (who was also a very successful author of musicals) wrote: 'The principle I always go on in writing a long story is to think of the characters in terms of actors in a play.' Plum explained that if he had a star to play a part he'd have to 'give him more to do and keep him alive till the fall of the curtain'.

He writes about readers' letters too ('I do grudge having to spend five cents on a letter to some female in East Grinstead who wants to know if I pronounce my name Wood-house or Wode-house'.

And then there is this, written in 1945 from a hotel in Paris: 'I was just writing this, when an air raid warning sounded. I thought all that sort of thing was over in Paris. Still, there it is. I will let you know how the matter develops.'

Enemy Coast Ahead
Guy Gibson VC
First published 1946

It is popular these days to sneer at the British bomber crews who, it can safely be argued, did more than anyone else to defeat Hitler and win World War II.

The sneering is largely done by people who seem to think it was perfectly acceptable for the Luftwaffe to bomb the life out of English cities (killing thousands of civilians in the process) but that it was somehow unreasonable for Britain to fight back.

The legendary Dam Busters raid on the Moehre-Eder dams was led by a young pilot called Guy Gibson, who was one of the greatest heroes of the war and a man whose raw courage gave hope to a beleaguered England and whose visit to America with Winston Churchill did much to bring that country into the war.

No one man did more to win the war than Guy Gibson. Sir Arthur Harris described him as 'as great a warrior as this island ever bred'. Barnes Wallis, inventor of the bouncing bomb described him as 'a man of great courage, inspiration and leadership'. And Winston Churchill, who regarded Gibson very highly, had hoped that Gibson would go into Parliament. (Gibson was selected for a seat in Macclesfield). 'His name will not be forgotten,' said Churchill,

It was Gibson who, having dropped his own bombs, circled the dams to distract the enemy, and draw their fire, while others completed the destruction. It was one of the most cleverly designed, accurate, thoroughly planned raids in military history and the damage it did to the German war effort was exceeded only by the boost it gave to the British morale.

Paul Brickhill's classic book 'The Dam Busters' describes what happened before and during the famous raid, but Gibson's autobiography gets my choice as the most personal account of the horror of the war.

Gibson, who was promoted to Wing Commander, could have easily sat out the war (and was ordered to do so) but he begged to be allowed to continue flying bombers. His last raid was a complete success but he never returned. He was killed in action. Guy Gibson was 26-years-old when he died and had completed 174 flying operations over Germany. He deserved a statue in central London every inch as tall as Horatio Nelson's.

It has been established that Gibson wrote his book himself, without a ghost writer.

Gibson was awarded the Victoria Cross, the Commander of the Legion of Merit (from the United States), the Distinguished Flying Cross and Bar and the Companion of the Distinguished Service Order and Bar.

A History of English Literature
John Buchan (Editor)
First published 1927
'A History of English Literature' gets very close to being either an encyclopaedia or a reference work of some variety. But I have over-ruled my own rule and included it because it is such a magnificent book.

John Buchan (the author of 'The Thirty Nine Steps' and, my favourite of his novels, 'John Macnab') edited this comprehensive volume – which only includes authors up to 1927, of course – but had help from a large number of eminent experts, critics and academics.

It is wonderfully comprehensive and I have, over the years, referred to it so often that my hardback copy is now, I confess shamefacedly, held together with a stout rubber band.

I bought a Mountain
T Firbank
First published 1940
I have a shelf full of books describing the adventures of people who

gave up conventional lives, ran away and bought or rented small farms, small holdings or, in at least one case, an island. They mostly wanted to lead simpler, less mentally stressful, more honest lives. Naturally, they all found that living in a remote cottage or farmhouse, struggling to make a living from the land, wasn't quite as easy as they'd hoped it would be. But they all learned a great deal about themselves and about life.

'I bought a mountain' was, I think, the first such book.

Firbank had been working in a factory in Canada when he heard about a sheep farm for sale in Wales. The farm, of 2,400 acres, included a house, two cottages and a variety of farm buildings and it was for sale for £5,000. Firbank, who had £5,000 in the bank, paid £4,625, leaving just enough to buy the stock. It was 1931.

The book's penultimate paragraph still strikes a chord today.

'Man are loath just now to return to the land. The life is hard, the wage small and the instinct of husbandry is dead in them. But man was born of husbandry. In the bleak times ahead he may turn again to his own sure helps, the soil. He will readjust his values and may taste in the end the ultimate joy of tending Nature in her labour.'

Amen.

As a writer I am proud to say that my winter greens, carrots, beans and beetroot are looking tolerably good.

Small is Beautiful
E.F.Schumacher
First published 1973

Fashionable, bestselling books are sometimes quickly forgotten – pushed aside by the 'something new', the author of the moment, the latest fad.

Tragically, this seems to be the case with Schumacher's book which was, when it came out, a huge bestseller and seemed destined to become a classic.

But the forces of globalisation were, perhaps, too much for it.

Schumacher argued, cogently and convincingly, that huge international corporations were inefficient and inhumane. He claimed that we would be better off with smaller businesses, using local resources and local labour. His thesis, well documented, was that smaller organisations were better for us all in every conceivable way. And he pointed out that we treat fossil fuels as an 'income item' when we should be using them as 'capital' and minimising their rate of use.

The final words of Schumacher's book are worth repeating here:

'Everywhere, people ask: 'What can I actually do?' The answer is as simple as it is disconcerting: we can, each of us, work to put our own inner house in order. The guidance we need for this work cannot be found in science or technology, the value of which utterly depends on the ends they serve: but it can still be found in the traditional wisdom of mankind.'

The Peter Principle
Dr Laurence J.Peter and Raymond Hull
First published in 1969

'The Peter Principle' is a very simple book because the underlying theory (the Peter Principle) is that people tend to be promoted until they reach a job they cannot really manage.

By then, of course, it is too late to do anything about them.

'The Peter Principle' helps explain why our parliaments are so badly run, why large businesses fail so often, why charities and trade unions are run diabolically and why schools and hospitals so often seem to be run by morons.

The theory partly explains why bridges so often collapse, why town planners build housing estates on flood plains, why, in 2021 the British Government wasted £4 billion buying personal protective equipment that was so useless that it had to be destroyed and lost £11 billion through a financial error. It explains why new cars are built with dangerous defects, why armies fight with equipment which doesn't do what it is supposed to do and why drugs and vaccines so often do more harm than good.

The Sense of Humour
Stephen Potter
First published 1954

Stephen Potter was the inventor of gamesmanship and the author of

'Gamesmanship', 'Lifemanship', 'One-Upmanship' and 'Supermanship'. It is not unreasonable, therefore, to assume that Mr Potter knows what is funny and what is not.

The first part of the book is an attempt to define the nature of humour. This section can, to be honest, be rather turgid and, dare I say it, humourless.

But the book comes to life in the main section which is full of examples of different types of funny writing.

Here is one of my favourites – taken I am afraid from one of James Agate's Ego diaries (which are also listed in this book). This was written in 1942.

'Eckersley told us how after the concert hall at Broadcasting House was built, there was doubt whether the door would admit a concert grand. 'Try it,' said somebody. But the music director objected on the ground that if his beautiful Bechstein got stuck it would be damaged. So they instructed the carpenter to take the measurements and make an exact replica in ply-wood. This was done, and they then found that they couldn't get the model out of the carpenter's shop.'

How to be an Alien
George Mikes
First published 1946

I worried for some time about whether or not this book should be included. My concern was inspired by the knowledge that 'How to be an Alien' is officially categorised as 'fiction'.

Eventually, I decided that so much of the book is accurate that I would reclassify it as a volume of social psychology and, therefore, non-fiction and, therefore, eligible for inclusion here. I think it is pretty certain that if the book had been published half a century later a publisher would have certainly listed it as non-fiction.

Mikes was a Hungarian who came to England and discovered that a foreigner can become British but he can never become English. (By the same token he can probably never become Scottish or Welsh.)

Mikes describes the trouble with tea, discusses the national passion for queuing, explains how to compromise, offers subtle advice on how the English are rude and points out that in England it is bad manners to be clever or to asset something, anything, with confidence.

And, inevitably, there is a section on how the English deal with the weather. 'In England,' says Mikes, 'you must be good at discussing the weather.'

Just why the publishers chose to classify this book as fiction is a complete mystery.

If you enjoy this book you will also enjoy Pierre Daninos' books about Major Thompson.

Adventures in the Screen Trade
William Goldman
First published 1983

William Goldman was the greatest screenwriter of the second half of the twentieth century. His film credits include 'Harper', 'All the President's Men', 'Butch Cassidy and the Sundance Kid', 'The Stepford Wives', 'A Bridge Too Far', 'A Few Good Men', 'Maverick', 'Absolute Power', 'Heat', 'The Hot Rock', 'Wild Card' and many, many more.

In addition, Goldman was the best writer about the movie business.

And, of the books he left us, this, the first, is probably the best.

Goldman loved movies. He'd have probably admitted that movies were his life, and he probably knew more about the business than anyone else.

He explains the star system ('stars are essentially worthless and absolutely essential'), treats us to wonderful titbits of gossip ('Bogart was described as a miserable pain in the ass and Cary Grant was convinced he had no charm'), gives us the low down on directors ('over the years I have met and worked with a dozen prize winning American directors, and there is not one whose 'philosophy' or 'world view' remotely interests me. The total amount of what they have to 'say' cannot cover the bottom of even a small teacup'), shares his views on producers ('like the goony-goony bird that flies in ever-decreasing circles until it gets swallowed up by its own asshole').

And there are wonderful hints on screenwriting.

I've just moved 'Adventures in the Screen Trade' from my book case full of movie books to my bookcase full of books to read again as soon as possible.

The Saturday Book No 17
Various authors
First published 1957

'The Saturday Book' was founded in 1941 and continued until 1975. Until I first saw a copy I assumed (for no good reason that I can think of) that 'The Saturday Book' consisted of syrupy poetry and twee articles of interest only to elderly maiden aunts taking time off from their knitting and looking for something to help them pass the time before the vicar came round. How wrong I was. I now have a collection which includes every edition of 'The Saturday Book' ever published. And, believe me, it wasn't easy to find the last one or two.

For all those years the editors succeeded in collecting contributions (articles, stories and art work) from the best writers of the day and from unknown writers with something useful to contribute. Each volume was beautifully illustrated with drawings and photographs.

For example, entirely at random, I just picked out the 17th edition which included articles and stories by Alan Ross, Roy Brooks, Miles Hadfield, Fred Bason (a wonderful discovery who tried to sell cigarette cards to Hitler and who then had most of his collection destroyed by one of Hitler's bombs) L.T.C.Rolt, Robert Gibbings, P.G.Wodehouse, Howard Spring and Peter Quennell with illustrations by, among others, David Gentleman, Osbert Lancaster, L.S.Lowry and Ronald Searle.

It didn't take me long to realise that 'The Saturday Book' was designed to be a treat for everyone, including elderly maiden aunts.

It was a sad day when the publishers stopped producing 'The Saturday Book'. Fortunately, there are a shelf full of Saturday Books for us to enjoy and many of them are still fairly easy to find. There are 34 volumes and a special edition called 'The Best of the Saturday Book' was published in 1981.

The Smith of Smiths
Hesketh Pearson
First published in 1934
Sydney Smith is remembered mainly for his bon mots and carefully crafted aphorisms. (Any decent dictionary of quotations will contain a good selection.)

Born in 1771, Smith was a clergyman who was much more than a man of the church. He was a farmer, a gardener and a cook and a man who acquired a thousand skills from a dozen professions. He was also a skilled journalist and essayist. And he was a friend of many – including Charles Dickens and Sir Robert Peel.

Smith retired to Combe Florey in the Somerset countryside (later famous as the home of Evelyn Waugh and then his son Auberon) which he found rather dull. 'I saw a crow yesterday,' he wrote, 'and had a distant view of a rabbit today'.

He didn't much like the countryside (despite being a farmer) and he wasn't too keen on old age. 'I am seventy two years of age…at which period there comes over one a shameful love of ease and repose, common to dogs, horses, clergymen and even to Edinburgh Reviewers. Then an idea comes across me sometimes that I am entitled to five or six years of quiet before I die. I fought with beasts at Ephesus for twenty years. Have I not contributed my fair share for the establishment of important truths, and for the discomfiture of quacks and fools? Is not the spirit gone out of me?'

It hadn't, of course.

Hesketh Pearson was one of the greatest of all biographers. He was also one of the most prolific. His biographies of Oscar Wilde, George Bernard Shaw and Conan Doyle are all well worth reading.

There have been a number of biographies of Sydney Smith (they're no doubt still coming) but Pearson's was so definitive as to make all others superfluous. Smith isn't going to produce any new aphorisms.

The Second Tree from the Corner
E.B.White

First published 1936
E.B.White is now perhaps best remembered for his two classics for children 'Charlotte's Web' and 'Stuart Little' but he was the most stylish of American essayists.

'E.B.White …says wise things gracefully,' 'said the New York Times, 'he is the master of an idiom at once exact and suggestive, distinguished yet familiar. His style is crisp and tender and incomparably his own.'

'The Second Tree from the Corner' contains essays first published in 'The New Yorker', 'Harper's' and 'Atlantic Monthly'.

Some of the essays are short, some longer, some (as with most really great essayists) tip toe round the edges of fiction, some are reports, some opinions, some about the past, some about the present and some about the future.

My favourite piece in this collection, entitled 'Farewell, My Lovely' is a beautiful memorial to the Model T Ford – an essay which was, at one time, published by itself as a small book.

A Journal of the Plague Year
Daniel Defoe
First published 1722
Daniel Defoe is credited with having invented the novel and his bestsellers 'Robinson Crusoe' and `Moll Flanders' are still hugely popular and now rightly regarded as classics. For his under-rated 'Memoirs of a Cavalier', Defoe invented the trick of pretending that he had discovered the manuscript among some old papers. (This, of course, is a trick that has been used many times since. George Macdonald Fraser used a similar ploy for his books about Flashman's adventures.)

Daniel Defoe's life was as packed with adventure as that of any storybook hero – including the hero of the novel 'Robinson Crusoe'. He was the world's first realistic novelist, a fearless political lobbyist, the world's first campaigning and investigative journalist and the publisher of one of the world's first newspapers. He was a merchant, a soldier and a tireless traveller and worked as a secret agent in Scotland for William III.

Born the son of a butcher in Stoke Newington, London, Daniel

Defoe travelled widely in Europe before setting up in the hosiery trade in London when he was just 23-years-old. He took part in Monmouth's rebellion and joined William III's army in 1688.

He began writing as a pamphleteer in 1691, and in 1697 he published An Essay Upon Projects which proposed paving the highways, enlarging the Bank of England, instituting friendly societies, reforming the bankruptcy laws and abolishing press gangs. He pleaded for the higher education of women and for a more humane treatment of lunatics. One of his satires resulted in a massive fine, a spell in the pillory and a term of imprisonment.

While in Newgate prison, Defoe continued to write pamphlets and on his release he founded a newspaper called 'The Review' which he wrote and published three times a week. 'The Review' included articles on political and domestic topics and introduced the idea of newspapers publishing leading articles and editorials.

While he was writing The Review (he wrote the whole of the paper himself) Defoe produced a vast number of pamphlets and a ghost story called The Apparition of One Mrs Veal which was, he claimed, a true account of something that had actually happened. (He realised even then that readers would enjoy a story much more if they believed it to be true. He did this by writing about believable characters in realistic situations and by using simple, easy to read prose. It was Defoe who invented the realistic novel.)

Defoe wrote an apparently endless number of pamphlets on a huge range of subjects, including travel, politics, religion, geography and the supernatural. Much of his political writing was in the form of satire and although he was popular with the public, he made a number of powerful enemies. The people in authority didn't like his attacking, fearless style.

Between 1704 and 1714, Defoe worked as a double agent and undertook a number of secret missions for the Tories. His sympathy was always with the outcasts and the failures. He wrote sympathetically about the consequences of the South Sea Bubble and he supported the starving hay-makers in 1722. He wrote an article attacking the practice of flogging in the army. He wrote about the return to England of transported felons.

Defoe's three greatest novels are undoubtedly The Life and Surprising Adventures of Robinson Crusoe, Moll Flanders and A Journal of the Plague Year (which was written as a diary and classified as non-fiction but was in fact a novel). The enormously successful and famous book about Robinson Crusoe was based on an interview Defoe did with a Scottish sailor named Alexander Selkirk, who had been shipwrecked for several years on a remote Pacific island.

While producing these remarkably successful novels, Defoe continued to write a huge variety of non-fiction. Between 1724 and 1727 he wrote an excellent three volume travel book called Tour through the Whole Island of Great Britain. His other non-fiction books included 'The Way to make London the Most Flourishing City in the Universe'.

He was a courageous man and an extraordinarily prolific and versatile author and by the time he died he had published more than 250 works. Every word he wrote was, of course, written out by hand.

There is no doubt that Defoe sometimes used his knowledge and skills for writing fiction to help with books which were originally classified as non-fiction and now, rather craftily, simply defined as 'literature'. All his books are important social histories as well as being eminently readable.

'The Journal of a Plague Year' is written in the first person and given that the plague years were 1664-1665 and that Defoe wasn't born until 1660, it is pretty clear that the Journal owed more than a little something to imagination.

But, I've classified it as non-fiction. The book was described by Anthony Burgess as 'the most reliable and comprehensive account of the Great Plague that we possess'.

Voyages and Discoveries of the English Nation
Hakluyt
First published 1589
Richard Hakluyt was an editor who, in the late part of the 16th century, collected together a number of document written by travellers and explorers and published them as 'The Principall Navigations, Voiages and Discoveries of the English Nation'.

The anthology included pieces describing journeys to the North East Passage, Persia, the Mediterranean, the Straits of Magellan, the Caribbean and Newfoundland.

Taken at random, the book includes the story of the first voyage of Master Martin Frobisher, searching for the strait or passage to China and the voyages of Master John Hawkins to the coast of Guinea and the Indies. And there is the original account of Drake's Circumnavigation (1577-1579) and the extraordinary story of the return of the first Muscovite ambassador from 1558 – which also includes astonishing descriptions of life in Russia with the Emperor.

It is the ultimate travel book, though now largely forgotten – perhaps because the title includes the word 'England'. It is, it seems, politically incorrect to mention English glories.

The Perfect Hostess
Rese Henniker Heaton
First published 1931

When I first found this book I half suspected that it was one of those spoofs which used to be popular and which are offered to the Christmas gift buying public looking for a novelty volume.

But it isn't. It's real and it's both charming and scarcely believable. At the front of the book is printed this motto: 'Il faut du temps pour etre Femme'.

The contents include advice on how to cope when: 'The woman your husband nearly married comes to lunch'; 'The Admiral, the General and the Retired Governor come to Luncheon'; 'Your poor relation comes up from the country for the day'; 'The flying ace comes to lunch before the big race'.

There are notes headed 'Little comforts for the bachelor's room', advice on travel entitled 'The intrepid traveller embarks for Calais' and advice on 'How to entertain a party of sub-lieutenants and junior midshipmen'. There are tips on 'Presents for the bridegroom costing less than two pounds' and vital advice for 'The perfect wife'.

Here are just a few of my favourite tips for when a burglar pays a midnight visit to your home

Take a tin can and kick it noisily down the stairs

If your husband insists on going to look for the burglar, see that he holds a poker in one hand and in the left hand a chair held upside down over his head to protect his skull

The author's other useful tips for women include putting a

gramophone in the bathroom (for guests who do physical exercises.) And she offers a draft letter to put off a guest who invites himself. To break the silence of an awkward pause she suggests saying the following: 'I think the plan of opening all the prisons and asylums next Sunday is a beautiful idea but I don't know how it will work out'.

And feminists everywhere will be delighted by this piece of advice: 'A wise woman will always let her husband have his way.'

Oh, and the advice for the hostess who has a friend from the tropics to stay includes: 'Put a copy of the Ceylon Times, Times of India and Singapore Times in his room. Don't feed him chicken on any account. Invite the young girls with the rosiest complexions to meet him.'

Absolutely, utterly brilliant.

The Shetland Bus
David Howarth
First published 1951

When Germany occupied Norway between 1940 and 1945, a constant stream of small boats travelled from the Shetland Isles to Norway. The boats landed weapons and supplies for the locals and helped rescue refugees.

The boat service became known as the Shetland Bus.

Sub Lieutenant David Howarth was the Royal Naval officer who had the responsibility of organising a base from the boats could operate.

When I was in my teens I pretty well knew this marvellous book by heart because it was one of the set books for my English literature 'O' level examination.

The fact that I still love the book should tell you everything you need to know about Mr Howarth's classic memoir of the Second World War, and of the courage of the intrepid, courageous sailors who operated the Shetland Bus.

My First book
Introduction by Jerome K.Jerome

First published 1894
The title says it all! What a brilliant and beautifully illustrated book this is. Twenty two authors explain how they came to write and publish their first book.

Robert Louis Stevenson explains that when planning 'Treasure Island' he had 'an idea for John Silver from which I promised myself funds of entertainment; to take an admired friend of mine…to deprive him of all his finer qualities and higher traces of temperament, to leave him with nothing but his strength, his courage, his quickness and his magnificent geniality…'.

There are contributions by (among others) Jerome K. Jerome, Rudyard Kipling, Conan Doyle, H.Rider Haggard, Marie Corelli, Hall Caine and R.M. Ballantyne.

It is a feast for any lover of books and authors.

The Book of Lists
David Wallechinsky, Irving Wallace, Amy Wallace
First published 1978
I thought long and hard about including this book because it is not what a lot of people would call a 'proper' book. But it is great fun and although it is inevitably a little out of date it's one of those books which are easy to pick up and damnably difficult to put down.

It is, as the title rightly suggests, nothing more than a book of lists. Here is my list of the book's greatest list headings:
10 of the worst generals in history
10 unexplored areas of the world
10 weapons named after people
10 doctors who tried to get away with murder
10 important libel cases
7 famous men who died as virgins
10 sensational thefts
9 breeds of dogs that bite the most
23 of the busiest lovers in history
14 worst human fears
10 worst films of all time
23 most boring jobs
At the back of the book there is a picture of Franz Liszt looking

very pleased with himself – as well he might.

Dr Dean Ornish's Program for Reversing Heart Disease
Dean Ornish
First published 1990
I have no idea how many practical medical books I have owned over the last six decades – many thousands certainly. Most of them have been given away to charity shops but I have always kept hold of this one which is one of the very best practical health books ever published.

Dr Ornish proved that heart disease can be halted or reversed simply by a change in lifestyle – following a vegan diet, taking modest exercise and controlling stress. His scientific studies produced astonishing results and at the end of a year most of the patients he treated reported that their chest pains had virtually disappeared; for 82% of the patients, arterial clogging had reversed.

Naturally, however, neither the medical profession not its controllers the pharmaceutical industry, took any notice. Surgeons continue to perform unnecessary operations and physicians continue to prescribe unnecessary (and harmful) drugs.

The book is still around, however, and it's as valid as ever.

A Writer Prepares
Lawrence Block
First published 2021
Lawrence Block has written too many excellent thrillers to count and has used so many pen names that I doubt if even he can keep track. Like many experienced and successful authors he chose to become an independent publisher (usually derided by industry dinosaurs as 'self-publishing') and is as successful at that as he is at writing wonderful books. Block is, without a doubt, one of the greatest modern American crime and thriller novelists.

Block has won multiple Edgar Allen Poe and Shamus awards and a UK Diamond Dagger for lifetime achievement and is a Mystery Writers of America Grand Master.

'A Writer Prepares' is a book about writing books, and Block explains how he became a professional writer and how he works on his books. He details his dealings with agents and his publishers and his friendships with other writers.

At the end of the book he explains that he chose to self-publish the memoir for two reasons: partly so that 'the text won't be filtered by any editorial sensibilities other than my own' and partly because, like all writers, he wants the book out quickly. 'When I finish a book, I want things to happen ASAP.'

Coaching Days and Coaching Ways
W.Outram Tristram
First published 1903
Mr Tristram succeeds in this book in capturing beautifully the essence of coach travel in England in the 19th century. His book describes in excellent detail the joys and menaces of travel along seven well used highways – The Bath Road, the Exeter Road, the Portsmouth Road, the Dover Road, the York Road and the Holyhead Road.

My copy (a first edition but not expensive) is illustrated with nearly 200 excellent line drawings by Hugh Thomson and Herbert Railton and contains a wealth of information about highwaymen, famous travellers and well-known hostelries where travellers stayed and fresh horses could be obtained.

'Coaching Days and Coaching Ways' is so full of detail that on reading it, it is possible to understand exactly what travel was like in days when a journey of just a hundred miles was uncomfortable but romantic and dangerous but exciting.

Today, in contrast, travel seems mostly just uncomfortable and boring.

The Kid Stays in the Picture
Robert Evans
First published 1994
Robert Evans played the Hollywood game by his own rules. He began life as an actor and the title of his autobiography comes from

the fact that the stars of the picture wanted him fired but the producer told them 'the kid stays in the picture'. He became a major producer at Paramount though he had very little experience. His first production was 'The Detective' starring Frank Sinatra, Lee Remick, Robert Duvall, Jacqueline Bisset and Jack Klugman. He was subsequently responsible for a mass of blockbuster films including 'The Godfather', 'The Godfather II', 'Love Story', 'True Grit', 'Serpico', 'The Odd Couple', 'Paper Moon', 'Marathon Man', 'The Italian Job', 'Chinatown' and 'Rosemary's Baby'. He had an ego slightly bigger than Mount Rushmore and the opening line of the book is brutally honest: 'There are three sides to every story: yours, mine and the truth.'

'The Kid Stays in the Picture' is a kiss and tell all memoir that itself begat a hugely popular movie and Evans, a man of seemingly infinite charm, and a friend of many Hollywood A listers, shares insider gossip with joy and a never ending sense of fun.

England My Adventure
Ethel Mannin
First published 1972

In a strange way, this is a love story since the driving force for the book is Ms Mannin's determination to visit places which mean something to her only because of the people with whom they have become associated.

And so (among others) she visits Ludlow because of A.E.Housman, Lichfield because of Dr Johnson, Nottingham for D.H.Lawrence, Haworth for the Brontes, Wigan for George Orwell, Farnham for William Cobbett and Selborne for Gilbert White.

In each town she relates her visit to the person with whom the town is connected. She searches out their homes, the public house they favoured, the town centre and so on. But it is much more than a series of homages because she vividly connects the places with her heroes and heroines, describes how the places have changed and looks at how they may change in the future.

It could have been turgid, a glorified guide book, a book with a manufactured theme. But it succeeds and is none of those things. It gives us a writer's eye view of England that will become part of

English social history.

English Journey
J.B.Priestley
First published 1934

I still love J.B.Priestley's novels, my favourites being 'The Good Companions', 'Festival at Farbridge' and 'Lost Empires' but although plays such as 'An Inspector Calls' survive, his fiction and non-fiction have all but disappeared, widely regarded as dated and frivolous.

Of his non-fiction this is the best by far. Priestley himself described the book as 'a rambling but truthful account of what one man saw and heard and felt and thought during a journey through England during the autumn of the year 1933'. Priestly wasn't the first to do it, of course. Celia Fiennes made a similar journey on horseback in 1698 and the book she wrote about her travels is almost as entertaining – but not quite.

The book fits Priestley's description precisely. (And how impressive it is that Priestley managed to complete the journey, write the book and get it published within 12 months.)

He starts his trip on a motor coach going to Southampton.

'I caught it with the minimum of clothes, a portable typewriter, the usual paraphernalia of pipes, notebooks, rubbers, paper fasteners, razor blades, pencils,' he began, 'Muirhead's, 'Blue Guide to England', Stamp and Beaver's 'Geographic and Economic Survey' and, for reading in bed, the tiny, thin paper edition of the 'Oxford Book of English Prose'.

After Southampton he travels to Bristol, to the Cotswolds, to Birmingham, Leicester and Nottingham and then North to West Riding, the Potteries, Lancashire and Durham and back down to Lincoln and Norfolk.

Mr Priestley sees much and tells us all he sees. It is, as are all the best travel books, a personal and opinionated account of his journey. It is at times depressing and at times cheerful but it is packed with social, industrial and political observations which enable us to understand England in the 1930s. Most important of all, however, it is as enthralling a read as any good novel. Mr Priestley can make the dullest town fascinating. 'English Journey' is a classic. Mr Priestley meets amusing people and sees odd things happening because he looks for them. There is fun and there are some saucy comments but the pace and interest never slackens for J.B.Priestly was a master wordsmith.

The Kon-Tiki Expedition
Thor Heyerdahl
First published 1950

The Kon-Tiki Expedition was the publishing sensation of my early boyhood, constantly reprinting and thrilling thousands of readers. I suspect that it pretty well saved its original publishers.

Heyerdahl began by wondering (as one does) about the mysteries of the South Seas and, more specifically, how the Polynesian race first crossed the Pacific Ocean.

Most of us, ordinary slipper owning mortals, would be content with wondering and dreaming and looking things up in books. Heyerdahl was not content with any of that. He had a theory that the South Americans travelled by raft, swept by currents and winds, and so he set out to test his theory. He found five companions by sending the following letter to some fellows he knew: 'Am going to cross the Pacific on a wooden raft to support a theory that the South Sea Islands were peopled from Peru. Will you come? I guarantee nothing but a free trip to Peru and the South Sea Islands and back, and you will find good use for your technical abilities on the voyage. Reply at once.'

If I'd sent such a letter I fear my friends would have had me locked away for my own safety.

But Heyerdahl's chums all accepted.

And so the six men (together with a parrot) built a raft with balsa logs and with a cabin made of bamboo. Their raft was an exact copy of old Indian vessels, with a single square sail between two masts lashed together.

And, with the aid of trade winds and Equatorial currents they proved that a South American balsa raft possesses amazing qualities and that the Pacific Islands lay well within the range of pre-historic rafts from Peru.

It is one of the great adventure stories of all time.

Confessions of an Opium Eater
Thomas de Quincey
First published 1822
De Quincey's 'Confessions of an Opium Eater' is the original 'I was a drug addict and (sort of) cured myself after many trials and tribulations', now so popular among book and newspaper publishers.

Here is de Quincey: 'And do I find my health after all this opium eating? In short, how do I do? Why, pretty well, I thank you, reader. In fact if I dared to say the real and simple truth (though in order to satisfy the theories of some medical men I ought to be ill) I was never better in my life than in the spring of 1812; and I hope sincerely that the qualities of claret, port, or London particular madeira which, in all probably you, good reader, have taken, and design to take, for every term of eight years during your natural life, may as little disorder your health as mine was disordered by all the opium I had taken (though in quantity such that I might well have bathed and swam in it) for the eight years between 1804 and 1812.'

De Quincey lived to be 74-years-old which, considering the amount of opium he used is quite impressive. He started taking opium to relieve the pain of facial neuralgia when he was a student at Oxford University.

The Last Grain Race
Eric Newby
First published 1956
At the age of 18, Eric Newby was working in an advertising agency. But then the agency lost an important cereal account and there were redundancies galore. Newby, however, was told that he was too unimportant (and cheap) to be sacked. He seethed as he travelled home on the underground. 'At Hammersmith, where I emerged sticky and wretched from the train, I found that we had been so closely packed that somebody had taken my handkerchief out of my pocket, used it and put it back under the impression that it was his own'.

The next day Newby went on holiday to Salcombe in Devon. On his way back to London, while waiting for a connection at Newton Abbott, he went into a café and applied for a job on a grain ship.

He signed on as an apprentice in a four-masted sailing ship for the round trip to Australia, to pick up a cargo of grain. It was 1938, and Newby had unknowingly signed on to sail in the last grain race to take place.

It was the first of Newby's many adventures on land and at sea.

The Armies of the Night
Norman Mailer
First published 1968

In October 1967, an anti-Vietnam demonstration was held in Washington. This is Mailer's account of the turmoil in America over that war. It is written, curiously, as a novel and with Mailer as a protagonist in a third person account.

I believe that two apparently small events helped end the Vietnam War.

The first was the arrest of Dr Benjamin Spock who was, the author of: 'Common Sense Book of Baby and Child Care' (a book which had sold over 50 million copies and was in as many American homes as the Bible and the Home Doctor). Spock was arrested and sentenced to two years in prison for his opposition to the Vietnam War. The sentence was later set aside. (The police should have learned from the experience of the French. In Paris, in 1968 the French police were told not to arrest Jean Paul Sartre when he took part in student demonstrations. The police in Paris obeyed their instructions and stood and watched as Sartre heaved cobble stones around.)

The second error occurred when two policemen threw Norman Mailer into the back of a prison van. (Mailer had almost certainly set out to be arrested.) Arresting Norman Mailer at a demonstration was disastrous, for Mailer then wrote his classic book 'The Armies of the Night' – which was at the time described as 'History as a Novel' and 'The Novel as History'.

The Years with Ross
James Thurber
First published 1957
I delighted in this book when it first came out. I had discovered Thurber very early in my life and much enjoyed both his writing and his cartoons.

But it was this memoir of his days at the New Yorker magazine and, in particular, of Harold Ross, the extraordinary editor of what was, at the time, the world's most readable magazine, which really fascinated me. Sadly, it has sunk very low in recent years and by the 21st century had become as readable as one of those free newspapers which local councils print and distribute (at great expense) to inform citizens of the joys of recycling or, perhaps, one of those free newspapers which are usually full of advertorials for double glazing. I hate to think what Ross would think of the magazine today.

When the eccentric and rather short-tempered Ross edited the New Yorker, his contributors included Robert Benchley, Dorothy Parker, Charles Addams, A.J.Liebling, Peter Arno and Alexander Woollcott. Ross edited in the style of an impresario, an old fashioned master of ceremonies, bringing in writers and illustrators as acts to entertain the magazine's weekly audience. But it was Thurber who made the New Yorker and no one could have written such an affectionate and yet revealing book about a magazine in its heyday.

In the end, Thurber began to lose his eyesight and he fell out of love with the magazine as subsequent editors tried (for no good reason that I can discern) to move the magazine on from its glory days.

American Notes & Pictures from Italy
Charles Dickens
First published 1842 and 1846
These two books are often published together (though heaven knows why – they are big enough to stand alone) and they are (together with Mark Twain's travel books) the very best of this kind of writing. (But, of course, they are. Dickens and Twain are arguably the two greatest writers in the English language.)

No one wrote more readable accounts of life on the road than

Dickens, the man who is (despite the sneers of modern literary critics who want Dickens, Shakespeare, Kipling, Buchan, Byron and Chaucer to be banned for being politically incorrect) still regarded by the truly discerning as the greatest of all novelists. At least one school exam board has thrown classic English poets out from their syllabus and replaced them with poets chosen for their skin colour. If I were wise I wouldn't include him in this book. After I wrote a book listing my favourite 100 Englishmen and Englishwomen, I was rather viciously attacked for including Charles Dickens, Winston Churchill, Lord Byron and William Shakespeare. These individuals are now proscribed by the censorious thought police. It sometimes seems to me as though every white, male author over 30-years-old, and certainly every dead male, white author, must be banned.

Only Dickens could turn a simple, ordinary encounter with a boot maker ('an artist in boots') into a scene worthy of an adventure in Pickwick Papers and only Dickens could describe across the Bridge of Sighs in Venice so vividly as to bring shivers to the spine of the reader.

Anyone who sneers at Dickens (and, sadly many do) knows nothing whatsoever about literature, books, people or great writing. So there, that's another bundle of abuse on social media!

The Servile State
Hilaire Belloc
First published 1913

I wasn't able to find my copy of 'The Servile State' so, since I knew I wanted to include it in this book, I had to purchase another. I now have two copies – one on my desk and one hiding somewhere. The only thing I know for certain is that I would not have given it away.

I've always enjoyed Belloc's work, ever since I read his 'Path to Rome' (which is only omitted from this collection because I decided that no one author would have more than one entry).

So what does Belloc mean by the 'servile state'?

Here is his definition: 'That arrangement of society in which so considerable a number of the families and individuals are constrained by positive law to labour for the advantage of other families and individuals as to stamp the whole community with the mark of such labour as we call the servile state.'

There can be no doubt: much of the world now consists of 'servile states'.

Here's how Belloc concluded his book (remember, he was writing in 1913): 'So far as I can judge, those societies which broke with the continuity of Christian civilisation in the 16th century – which means, roughly, North Germany and Great Britain – tend at present to the re-establishment of a servile status. It will be diversified by local accident, modified by local character, hidden under many forms. But it will come.'

And it came.

Biography
Vernon Coleman

Sunday Times bestselling author Vernon Coleman qualified as a doctor in 1970 and has worked both in hospitals and as a principal in general practice. Since 1975, he has written over 100 books which have sold over two million copies in the UK and been translated into 26 languages. Several of his books have been on the bestseller lists. He has written over 5,000 articles in national newspapers and magazines and has presented numerous programmes on television and radio. His novel Mrs Caldicot's Cabbage War was turned into an award winning movie. Vernon Coleman is a bibliophile and has a large library. Since 1999 he has been very happily married to the artist, Donna Antoinette Coleman, with whom he has co-written five books. They live in the delightful if isolated village of Bilbury in Devon where they have designed for themselves a unique world to sustain and nourish them in these dark and difficult times.

Note from the Author:
If you found this book informative I would be very grateful if you would put a suitable review online. It helps more than you can imagine. If you disliked the book, or disapproved of it in any way, please forget you read it.
Vernon Coleman

Printed in Poland
by Amazon Fulfillment
Poland Sp. z o.o., Wrocław
21 November 2022

801ef707-272b-4f8b-9831-b71c0820d691R01